FULMAX POWER HAMMER

The custom Power Hammer for the 21st century. This power hammer has been designed by Loren Richards and built from the ground up as an update to the classic power hammer design. The FULMAX Model LR-30 proof of concept has been running and extensively tested for the past three years.

Designed with input from some of the world's best metal shaping artists and professionals, the FULMAX has been designed to eliminate some of the inherent flaws of the original power hammers.

Features:
- Quick Change Dies
- Rounded dies for more cost effective manufacturing
- Variable Frequency Drive speed control
- Rotating mass aligned with support beam; no more "side shake"
- Steel reinforced concrete main column
- Fully adjustable stroke and shut height
- Commercial grade at a reasonable price

MADE IN THE USA

FULMAX POWER HAMMER
TOOLS FOR SHAPING, LLC
A DIVISION OF FULTON METAL WORKS
www.toolsforshaping.com

Turn your HOBBY into a CAREER

Two training options to become an Automotive Collision Repair & Refinishing Technician

Located in Cleveland, WI
Lakeshore Technical College has
created cutting-edge Automotive programs that
get you ready to launch a great career in an in-demand field.

SHORT-TERM AUTO COLLISION REPAIR PROGRAM
- Get the skills you need for job entry into auto body metal finishing and painting
- Courses cover welding, panel replacement, metal forming, sheet metal alignment and refinishing

2-YEAR AUTOMOTIVE COLLISION REPAIR & REFINISHING TECHNICIAN PROGRAM
- Hands-on experience with metal forming and welding
- Automotive painting
- Latest repair methods using best equipment available
- Learn aluminum repair and collision repair for hybrid and electric vehicles

Apply today! gotoltc.edu/Auto

NEW AUTO COLLISION TRAINING CENTER OPENS FALL OF 2017!

NEW Power Hammer allows students to take plain sheets of aluminum or steel and form car or airplane parts—even complete car bodies!

LAKESHORE TECHNICAL COLLEGE
1.888.GO TO LTC
1290 North Avenue • Cleveland WI
NCA-Accredited ncahlc.org

This program is accredited by the National Automotive Technicians Education Foundation

Power Hammers
Using the Ultimate Sheet Metal Fabrication Tool

William H. Longyard

Published by:
Wolfgang Publications Inc.
P.O. Box 223
Stillwater, MN 55082
www.wolfpub.com

Legals

First published in 2015 by Wolfgang Publications Inc., P.O. Box 223, Stillwater MN 55082

© William H. Longyard, 2015

All rights reserved. With the exception of quoting brief passages for the purposes of review no part of this publication may be reproduced without prior written permission from the publisher.

The information in this book is true and complete to the best of our knowledge. All recommendations are made without any guarantee on the part of the author or publisher, who also disclaim any liability incurred in connection with the use of this data or specific details.

We recognize that some words, model names and designations, for example, mentioned herein are the property of the trademark holder. We use them for identification purposes only. This is not an official publication.

ISBN 13: 978-1-929133-60-4

Printed and bound in U.S.A.

On the cover: Two men working together to bring power hammers back into more common use by industry as well as small fab and customizing shops. On the left, Chris Rusch, designer of the power hammers and E-wheels manufactured by his company: RMD. On the right, Mr. power hammer, Mark Gerisch, the man who road tests Chris' new hammer designs, putting them through their paces before they go to production.

Power Hammers

Chapter One
Hammer Times — *Page 8*

Chapter Two
The Marketplace — *Page 14*

Chapter Three
1939 GMC Door — *Page 22*

Chapter Four
From Plainfield to Pebble Beach — *Page 36*

Chapter Five
Three Machines -
One Perfect Part — *Page 56*

Chapter Six
The Academy for the
Art of Metal Shaping — *Page 62*

Chapter Seven - Part 1
AAMS Students -
Speed Build a Ferrari 250 GTO — *Page 68*

Chapter Seven - Part 2
AAMS Students - Upper Fender — *Page 75*

Chapter Seven - Part 3
AAMS Students - Fender Reverse — *Page 78*

Chapter Seven - Part 4
AAMS Students -
Lower Cheek Fabrication — *Page 84*

Chapter Seven - Part 5
AAMS Students - Ferrari Cowl — *Page 86*

Chapter Seven - Part 6
AAMS Students - Lower Nose — *Page 90*

Chapter Eight - Part 1
More Cobra Panels
Mark Gerisch — *Page 94*

Chapter Eight - Part 2
The Other Headlight Panel — *Page 100*

Chapter Eight - Part 3
A Metal Medley — *Page 106*

Chapter Nine
A Flare for Metal — *Page 112*

Chapter Ten
Saving Edison's Car — *Page 122*

Chapter Eleven
Art Rods — *Page 134*

Chapter Twelve
Power Driven — *Page 142*

Chapter Thirteen
Homemade Diamond Plate — *Page 154*

Chapter Fourteen
Welding What You Hammer — *Page 162*

Sources/Catalog — *Page 172*

Acknowledgements

THE GOLDEN AGE OF METAL SHAPING

When I was a kid back in the 1960s it was common to hear some old timer rap his knuckles on the thin metal of a new car and dismissively grumble, *"They don't build'em like they used to!"* He was right of course. The cars of the 1960s were infinitely better than the cars of the '20s and '30s!

It's common amongst oldsters to claim the past was better than the present, and I'm guilty of doing that too at times. However, when it comes to metal shaping, the times have never been better than now. We are in a golden age of metal shaping, a renaissance is happening all around us. Back in the 1960s and '70s the Great Depression and WWII generation of metal shapers were beginning to retire, and as they did, they were taking the secrets of the trade with them. That generation rarely shared their knowledge because hoarding metal knowledge was the best way to ensure you remained employable. Your skills fed your family. If you gave your craft secrets away your value diminished.

But times changed and in the 1980s and '90s a handful of shapers began to produce books and videos describing the nearly lost art of metal shaping. They found a small, but very hungry audience. In the last twenty years, and especially since the advent of social media, metal shaping as a profession and avocation has come roaring back and now thousands of well-networked people around the globe have joined together to share their knowledge, share their techniques, and share the pure joy of shaping metal. This book would not have been possible without the generous contributions of the craftsmen presented here who shared their knowledge so freely. The torch of panel beating has been passed to a new generation. Let it shine brightly forever.

Dedication

No matter where I travel in America visiting great metal shapers and coachbuilders, often when I ask them how they got started in metal work -there is one name they mention with admiration and appreciation- *Ron Fournier*. Ron's 1982 ***Metal Fabricator's Handbook*** got many of us launched into this wonderful world of panel craft and fabrication, and so this book is for you Ron. Thanks from all of us!

Ron Fournier, who launched a thousand metal shaping careers with his highly influential Metal Fabricator's Handbook, has just autographed my personal copy which I purchased in 1982.

Foreword

Welcome to the revolution! Lately a new generation of shop and wallet friendly power hammers has come along and these have opened up the world of panel craft to a young generation of shapers who might never have afforded the old legacy machines like Yoders and Pettingells. Those venerable old work horses gave America, and the world, wings and wheels back in the day when movies were black & white, and telephones hung on a wall, not in a pocket. The new power hammers are faster, smaller, cheaper, and much easier to use, and that's exciting.

Although I started on those old-style machines, I've embraced the new ones and have chosen, at this point in my career, to embark on a new path, one in which I pass on my skills and experience to the next generation of metal shapers. These young men and women will have a much easier time learning the craft than I did thanks to books like this one, YouTube, Instagram, and the availability of this new generation of tools.

A modern power hammer can fit in a small shop and allows the solo craftsman to turn out a volume of work that used to require several craftsmen. With a modern power hammer, and the right instruction, *a one man shop can be profitable.*

I tell the students in my academy that it's a great time to become a coachbuilder. I invite you to consider learning this trade which has brought so many blessings to me.

Hammer on!

Mark Gerisch

Director
Academy for the Art of Metalshaping
Green Bay, Wisconsin

Chapter One

Hammer Times

If I had a Hammer

The idea for a power hammer first occurred to a weary Chinese grain farmer about 2,000 years ago. In the days before aspirins and workman's comp, ancient texts record that a lever-like device, probably foot powered, was used to crush grain. This mechanized hammer superseded the hand operated mortar and pestle and thus saved the Asian farm worker time, effort, and trips to the acupuncturist to relieve tendonitis.

By the golden age of Greece, lever-armed hammers were powered by rotating water wheels and hammered more than just rice and cereals. Now called trip hammers due to the use of a cam wheel to raise and suddenly drop the lever, the machines became the very first powered metal working tools. Trip hammers were invaluable

This huge martinet was built in Lyon, France in 1946. It is still used there by one of Europe's most prolific coachbuilders Mohamed Awadi. Mohamed plans to open a coachbuilding shop and school in his native Tunisia soon.

Victorian era trip hammers used steam power and could forge heavy bars of iron. Note the spare cam wheel on the right. Diorama in the Deutsches Museum, Munich.

When the French beat out the copper sheets to form the Statue of Liberty's cladding in the early 1880s, they used hand mallets over wood lath bucks. Very soon, however, as sheet metal became more and more common, smaller trip hammers were developed. Tool innovation accelerated in the 1890s with the advent of automobiles, and the requirements for mass production. In Europe large trip hammers shrunk into "helve" hammers (northern when forging metal ingots into usable bars and rods, but also when thinning, or forming, sheet metal. Some of these tools were small enough to be used in local blacksmith shops, while others were so huge they required gangs of dozens of strong men to manipulate the huge red hot bars of iron they forged. Looking today at nineteenth century pictures of these men and machines in fiery, smoky, locomotive works, the gargantuan arm pounding, sparks flying, no protective clothing whatsoever- is a sobering vision of Victorian industrial hell.

But the power hammer made hard work easier, and as the nineteenth century progressed and iron and casting technology became much cheaper almost any small-town smithy could afford a little power hammer in his shop. A blacksmith's hammer, often mounted on a wooden post, could quickly rough out horseshoes, as well as bars, rod stock, and other shapes, all while saving the smith's wrists, arms, and elbows from the early onset of arthritis. Small power hammers were truly lifesavers in a world without disability insurance.

Even small blacksmith shops in the US could afford machines like this Little Giant. Well over 100 years old, and originally belt powered, it is still used by the Mystic Seaport Museum in Connecticut. Photo courtesy Ed Crotty.

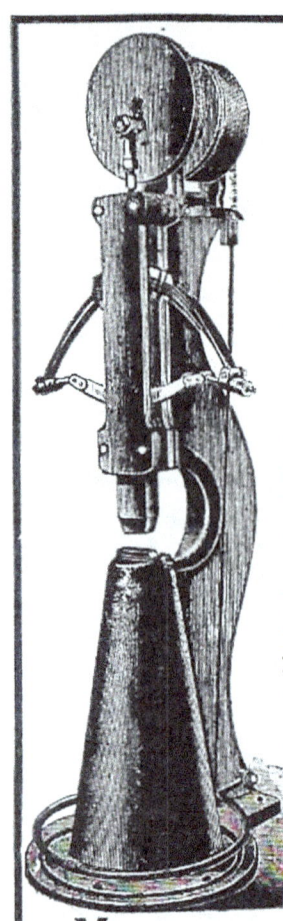

By 1914 blacksmiths, and others, had turned to coachbuilding for the auto-trade. Pettingell's could be mounted on any barn post and were light-duty enough not to shake the building down.

Europe), "martinets" (France), and "maglios", Italy. In the US, companies like Pettingell and Yoder added longer arms to the familiar post-mounted blacksmith power hammer so it could work deeply into a panel.

WHIP IT GOOD

From ancient times up until the late 1900s "power hammers" could only impart the force of the blow created by dropping a certain weight from a certain height. Gravity determined power. Trip hammers, drop hammers, and other similar tools, needed weight to be powerful. In Europe hammers were developed with a long slender arm of flexible hardwood which, when raised quickly, stored potential energy as it rose, and released that energy in a whipping action as it suddenly came down. The word "martinet" in French means "whip", and by coincidence, is closely related to

The mighty Yoder power hammer of WWII. These brutes were strong enough to crown several aluminum aircraft panels at a time. Note the leaf spring above the top die..

Stanguellini's carrozzeria late '40s showing a two meter long maglio in the back. All the little Modenese racers, like this 1100, were built using this type of power hammer.

the French word for hammer, "marteau". Wooden armed helves, martinets, and maglios are actually *whipping* machines. They are much more powerful than earlier trip hammers, even though usually smaller.

Similarly, in the US post-mounted hammers at this time gained a spring mechanism between the lifting pinion and the tooling which created a whipping action. In addition to the benefit of storing energy, wooden arms and metal springs allowed for an "over-stroke" to occur without shredding the sheet metal being worked. In other words, the tool could contact the sheet metal before the vertical plunge of the tool is complete, but the spring then soaks up the over-stroke without destroying the panel, or over-stressing the machine's pivot points. The springing effect acts as a power governor.

It is important to understand that *in today's parlance*, a POWER HAMMER is almost always considered a machine that has some amount of whipping action. Machines where the tooling is solidly connected to the actuating mechanism are usually considered RECIPROCATING MACHINES. Generally speaking, *power hammers* are more powerful and useful in shaping sheet metal while *reciprocating machines* are more useful in adding panel detail.

Sean O'Harra's beautiful restoration of a century old French ELWOR martinet he imported..

11

Understanding the Difference

The English wheel Vs. the power hammer, linear stretching vs. radial stretching. The whole discussion can at times be like talking to some one who is hung up on the old Ford Vs. Chevy argument. Lets look at what the differences are because many people would not have such strong opinions between them if they only knew what both do to metal when shaping.

First, let's look at the English wheel; although the E-wheel may look simple, as there are only two moving parts, I can assure you that there is more to it than that. When I started out, like most people, my first 10 years were spent on the E-wheel. During that time I became well versed at getting the shapes I wanted in a panel - and at getting rid of too much shape as well. My old friend, Lawrence Kett of G & A Fabrications, located at Walton on Thames in England befriended me during my first visit to England when I stopped by AC Cars. He and his wonderful family took me in and spent a great deal of time helping me understand the E-wheel. A brilliant craftsman, Lawrence showed me the way when others in this country would not. Look his workshop up at www.ga-fabrications.com

After fabricating many successful creations using the E-wheel I found later that the techniques needed to operate an English wheel are as vast as you can imagine. But there is one thing I was taught by Lawrence that was paramount in shaping with an E- Wheel properly. That is to always wheel in the same direction back and fourth without any cross wheeling where you would change the orientation of the panel 90 degrees. Cross wheeling opens you up to a myriad of problems in the panel, from marks that will not come out, to making your panel appear wavy, to hard spots that can build up tension and get trapped in the panel making it very difficult to relieve for a smooth looking panel.

Imagine the panel you are about to shape as it comes from the mill. Think of the molecules that make up the sheet as BBs, all comfortably aligned to each other. The molecular structure of the BBs changes with every hit, shrink, and track from an E-wheel - all of which make the panel stiffer than when it came to you. When you start tracking a panel on the E-wheel to get the desired shape, continuous lines of tension are placed in the panel making it very rigid. If you take note of someone shaping a panel using an E-wheel, you will see that the panel always maintains the shape and direction of what the final part is intended to be. I.E. a front fender will always look like a front fender, from start to finish, for whatever you are making. Nothing is wrong with that and one cool part is the way the highly polished upper and lower wheels will give the metal, especially aluminum, a burnished, or polished look.

The problem comes when the panel is welded. With so much tension, the panel will often pull and shrink along your weld-affected zone - sometimes making it look wavy. When fabricators see this they think they've ruined the panel. In fact, all they need to do is crush the weld itself to bring the panel back to its original, intended look.

Too many times people see the shrink waves created by the heat and start addressing the waves; this is when the real trouble starts. Stay on the weld, get it smooth, and then address areas that may still be a bit wavy.

Understanding the Difference

Today, I only use the English Wheel for a few things that I find it does very, very well. One is a series of wash-over passes when planishing will not get out the little waves in the surface that the hammer might leave. The other is when the E-wheel is fitted with a rubber top wheel with a fairly high durometer rating, meaning that during the back and forth passes, the lower anvil wheel will put a valley in the panel without doing any stretching. It's a nice way to put the finishing touches on a beautifully shaped panel.

Now the power hammer, which differs dramatically from the English Wheel because it shapes the metal in a radial fashion, round, instead of a straight, narrow linear lines. This is so much better for what you are trying to create with a sheet of metal that it is on a completely different level. There is very little tension in a panel that has been created using a power hammer because it spreads the struck area out in 360-degree pattern with every hit. Radial shaping with the hammer is like dropping a pebble in a pond, the ripple effect travels through the sheet evenly without building tension and it doesn't matter what direction you move when you're shaping. From side to side, front to back or just a small area that needs to be lifted, the effect leaves the metal sheet in a floppy, but correctly shaped condition, the way the sheet came to you from the mill. The BBs, (or molecules), are all still in alignment and happy to be where they are.

When it comes to welding a panel that has been shaped and/or shrunk using a power hammer you will get far less distortion, if any, because the panel isn't under tension. Although this machine can look very daunting and complex, with all its moving parts and settings, it is much easier to use and more intuitive to learn, than the E-wheel. Another bonus is the fact that you can shape multiple pieces at one time. So, if you're making a part, and you really need more than one, just stack two (or even three) sheets together and start shaping. You can at least rough them all out at one time, something you cannot do with the E-wheel.

Some people feel that it doesn't matter how you got the intended shape you were after - with an E-wheel or power hammer - as long as you get the correct shape. But after 35 plus years in this trade I can, without reservation, tell you the outcome is as different as the journey you took to get there. Most notably when the panels are welded together as the part is put into service.

There is so much more to understand about the uses of the two machines that it would be impossible for me to write them down in the space we have. I urge you to take some classes-from reputable coachbuilders who understand these two machines and can help you to achieve your potential with each machine. If you can't find someone that knows them both very well as I do then you may need to find teachers that know one or the other as long as you find them both, so you can make an informed decision yourself.

I wish you all the best in your endeavors and keep the art of Couch Building and metal shaping alive for others as well as yourself.

Mark Gerisch
AAMS President/Master CoachBuilder

Chapter Two

The Marketplace

Not Your Father's Power Hammer

The power hammer today is enjoying a renaissance. Metalshaping as a marketable skill has rebounded thanks to the explosion in classic car values the past few years and the need to produce panels for which replacements are no longer available. There is also a large surge of interest in coachbuilding as a hobby. Professionals who start out on English wheels often are forced to add a hammer to their shop simply to increase production and stay competitive. For hobbyists, the falling price of hammers, and especially the home garage-friendly size of many of the new ones, makes them an attractive, and even fun, upgrade to home shops.

The Baileigh MH-37HD is the most functional and efficient power hammer ever designed. It speeds production and is much easier to learn and master than legacy Yoders or Pettingells. Here, power hammer master Mark Gerisch puts the prototype through its paces.

When your slide strap breaks on your legacy machine, be sure to have one of these spring compressors so you can renew it.

However, even in those two extreme instances there is now a modern hammer that can do the same heavy duty work more quickly and more easily. I'm referring to the awesome Baileigh MH-37HD which you will read about later in this chapter. For the vast majority of craftsmen who are making automobile, truck, or aircraft panels, however, a somewhat smaller machine is adequate.

Another reason that I discount the legacy machines is that their prices have greatly inflated the past ten years or so. An ex-rust belt factory power hammer built, say, in 1940, used to sell for $10,000-$15,000. Those machines now routinely go for $50,000-$75,000, and often in a condition that requires a rebuild.

In the past the two main power hammer manufacturers were the American companies Yoder and Pettingell. Though Pettingell is a memory, Yoder hammers on, even though they've only sold one hammer in the last decade. It had to be fabricated from plate because they had lost the castings for their original machines! Today their business is mostly roll forming equipment.

There is nothing wrong with the big legacy machines of the past and hundreds of them thunder on each day around the globe shaping beautiful panels as you will see in subsequent chapters. But times have changed, and the new generation of power hammers offer so many advantages over the time-honored old ones I can see no reason for most shops to even consider purchasing a used Yoder or Pettingell. Let me be clear...*most shops*. There are certain applications where a large, 19th century style machine could be an option. I'm thinking of the custom boat-building industry where some large private yacht hulls are skinned in 1/4" (6mm) aluminum plate. Another application might be custom architectural work.

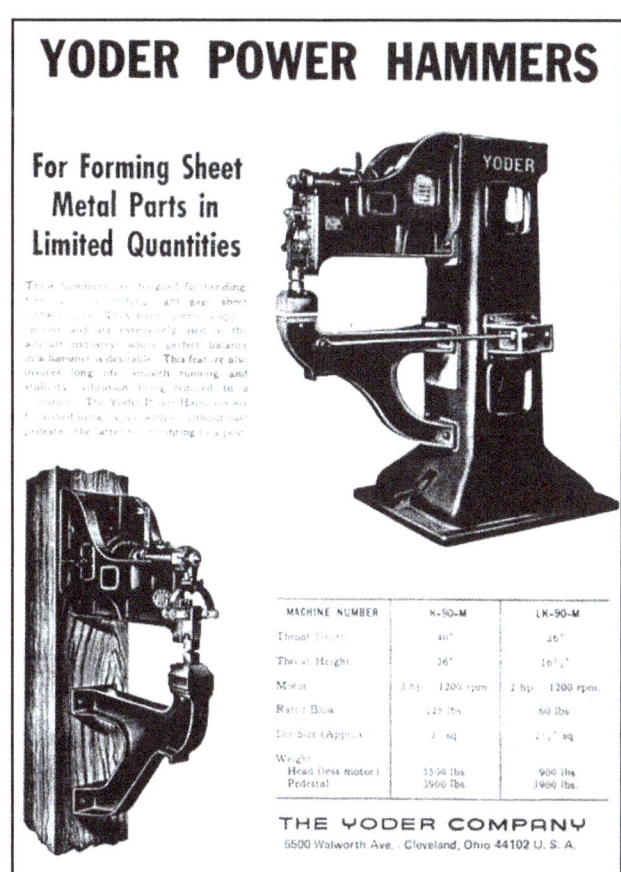

Developed in the age of the Model T, Yoder hammers face tough competition today from easier to use and less expensive machines. This ad is circa 1950.

15

Somewhat surprisingly vintage power hammers are now "collectible" and people with high-end car collections now see a perfectly restored and pin-striped Pettingell in the corner as a status symbol.

I can see no reason for anyone who intends to make money with a power hammer to bid against a well-heeled antique machinery collector when brand new machines are better, easier to use, and cost a lot less.

Power Hammers
Yoder

The company today offers only one hammer, the K-90-M, which in external appearance is similar to their great power hammers of yesteryear, but is no longer made from castings. It is now made from fabricated steel plate, which to

Machine designer Chris Rusch discusses the advantage of his MH-19 with recent convert from legacy machines, Danny Pascoe.

me, is a sensible improvement both in cost and durability. Powered by a 1,200RPM electric motor with a cone clutch, this machine utilizes the same 3"(78mm) square tooling of older machines, and carries on the Yoder tradition of quality that metalshapers have trusted for well over one-hundred years.

The Powell Hammer

Steve Powell in Michigan offers custom-built Yoder and Pettingell clones that go beyond merely replicating the look of the legacy machines, they actually are improvements on the old designs. Steve works with customers one at a time and tweaks each hammer to fit the customer's exact needs. The most obvious improvement of a Powell hammer is that it can fit in a shop with an 8 foot (2,500mm) ceiling. Additionally, his steel fabricated hammers weigh only one third that of a cast Yoder and are easily dismantled. The fact that Steve himself works with each customer before and after the sale is an important reason to consider his products.

Mittler Brothers

Mittler offers a range of smaller power hammers that make a lot of sense to someone on a

Steve Powell Yoder clone. A significant improvement and customizable.

Kyle Yocum tries the MH-37HD for the first time.

Baileigh MH-37HD

Hands down the greatest power hammer ever. Designer Chris Rusch took all of the attributes of his MH-19 and scaled them up to create this extremely powerful yet easy to operate machine which can bend metal as well as any of the biggest legacy machines. No other machine on the market offers the power, speed of adjustment, motor control, or flexibility of the MH-37HD. It features "Pullmax mode" too. This is a breathtaking machine in use, but aimed at busy production shops, or those working on heavy duty projects. It is more than most coachbuilders need, but even they could benefit from its ability to shape metal faster than even the MH-19. Very much a dream machine.

tight budget or in a confined area. Their designs are akin to early post-mounted Pettingells, but are powerful enough to perform any coachbuilding or airframe job. The company offers the buyer anything from parts kits to complete hammers, and at very reasonable prices. They also market an excellent range of affordable dies.

Baileigh MH-19

Designed and built by RMD and marketed by Baileigh, this machine is nothing short of brilliant and the first real improvement in power hammer design since electric motors replaced overhead leather belt drive 100 years ago. The attributes of this machine are many, but the highlights include: Easily fits in any 8 foot (2,500mm) room; easily moved with a pallet jack; no tools needed to adjust post height or power stroke; instant die change; foot pedal VFD speed control; instant convertibility to a reciprocating machine ("Pullmax mode"); rugged billet and plate construction; and, most importantly, completely made-in-the-USA factory support. Most of the craftsmen in this book use the MH-19 and for good reason.

A clever and compact design, the new Fulmax LR 30.

Fulmax LR 30

Another great leap forward in hammer design comes from the highly respected team of Loren Richards and Stan Fulton. Starting with a clean sheet of paper, Loren, the designer, worked to eliminate all the drawbacks of the legacy machines, the two biggest of which are their height and the hassle of tool changes. By reorienting the rotational mass 90° to the machine's axis, vibration is minimized during hammer strokes which allows the use of a much lighter column which is made from reinforced concrete instead of plate steel. Quick tool changes, coil springs, and VFD speed drive are other improvements. The machine can fit in an 8 foot (2,500mm) room and is very affordable. I believe that

Ron Covell really likes his Dake H100.

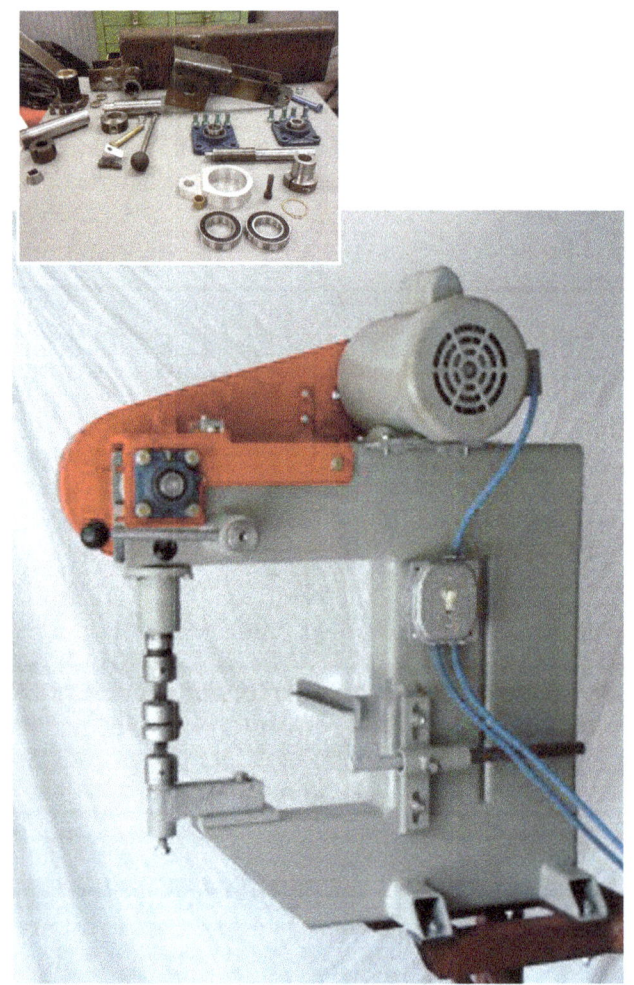

Shop Dog plans are available for free. Inset: Mark Stuart used them to build his own machine.

customer care after the sale is an important consideration for power hammer purchasers and over the years Stan, who manufactures the machine, has earned high praise for his products and service, something to which I can personally attest.

RECIPROCATING MACHINES

The Pullmax line of reciprocating machines were designed in Sweden and their initial purpose was to cut sheet metal blanks using shearing or nibbling die sets. Pullmax, which used to be part of the ESAB group of companies, built about 50,000 of their machines in several sizes before the advent of CNC cutters made them obsolete. A few other companies, like Trumpf in Germany, built similar machines and even today new Pullmaxes are available under the brand name Pull-X.

As big shops sold off their old Pullmaxes in the 1980s small shops and amateur coachbuilders discovered that Pullmaxes fitted with shrinking dies could be used as make-shift power hammers. Small shops now had a machine that could stretch, shrink, planish, and bead panels all at knock-down, fire sale prices due to the shrinkage of manufacturing in the U.S. and Europe.

In the early 2,000s, the advent of motorcycle and hot rod reality shows on TV introduced mil-

Kyle Yocum tries the MH-37HD for the first time.

Baileigh MH-37HD

Hands down the greatest power hammer ever. Designer Chris Rusch took all of the attributes of his MH-19 and scaled them up to create this extremely powerful yet easy to operate machine which can bend metal as well as any of the biggest legacy machines. No other machine on the market offers the power, speed of adjustment, motor control, or flexibility of the MH-37HD. It features "Pullmax mode" too. This is a breathtaking machine in use, but aimed at busy production shops, or those working on heavy duty projects. It is more than most coachbuilders need, but even they could benefit from its ability to shape metal faster than even the MH-19. Very much a dream machine.

tight budget or in a confined area. Their designs are akin to early post-mounted Pettingells, but are powerful enough to perform any coachbuilding or airframe job. The company offers the buyer anything from parts kits to complete hammers, and at very reasonable prices. They also market an excellent range of affordable dies.

Baileigh MH-19

Designed and built by RMD and marketed by Baileigh, this machine is nothing short of brilliant and the first real improvement in power hammer design since electric motors replaced overhead leather belt drive 100 years ago. The attributes of this machine are many, but the highlights include: Easily fits in any 8 foot (2,500mm) room; easily moved with a pallet jack; no tools needed to adjust post height or power stroke; instant die change; foot pedal VFD speed control; instant convertibility to a reciprocating machine ("Pullmax mode"); rugged billet and plate construction; and, most importantly, completely made-in-the-USA factory support. Most of the craftsmen in this book use the MH-19 and for good reason.

A clever and compact design, the new Fulmax LR 30.

Fulmax LR 30

Another great leap forward in hammer design comes from the highly respected team of Loren Richards and Stan Fulton. Starting with a clean sheet of paper, Loren, the designer, worked to eliminate all the drawbacks of the legacy machines, the two biggest of which are their height and the hassle of tool changes. By reorienting the rotational mass 90° to the machine's axis, vibration is minimized during hammer strokes which allows the use of a much lighter column which is made from reinforced concrete instead of plate steel. Quick tool changes, coil springs, and VFD speed drive are other improvements. The machine can fit in an 8 foot (2,500mm) room and is very affordable. I believe that

Ron Covell really likes his Dake H100.

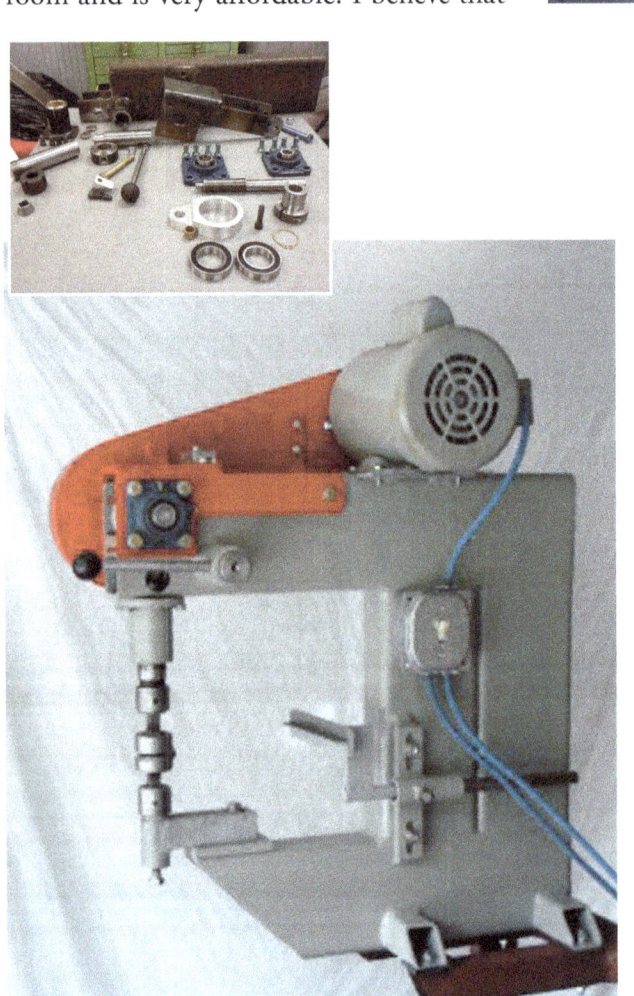

Shop Dog plans are available for free. Inset: Mark Stuart used them to build his own machine.

customer care after the sale is an important consideration for power hammer purchasers and over the years Stan, who manufactures the machine, has earned high praise for his products and service, something to which I can personally attest.

RECIPROCATING MACHINES

The Pullmax line of reciprocating machines were designed in Sweden and their initial purpose was to cut sheet metal blanks using shearing or nibbling die sets. Pullmax, which used to be part of the ESAB group of companies, built about 50,000 of their machines in several sizes before the advent of CNC cutters made them obsolete. A few other companies, like Trumpf in Germany, built similar machines and even today new Pullmaxes are available under the brand name Pull-X.

As big shops sold off their old Pullmaxes in the 1980s small shops and amateur coachbuilders discovered that Pullmaxes fitted with shrinking dies could be used as make-shift power hammers. Small shops now had a machine that could stretch, shrink, planish, and bead panels all at knockdown, fire sale prices due to the shrinkage of manufacturing in the U.S. and Europe.

In the early 2,000s, the advent of motorcycle and hot rod reality shows on TV introduced mil-

Jeb Greenstone's nicely restored Pullmax. You need ample shop space for one of these.

lions of wannabe metalshapers to the wonders of Pullmaxes and all of a sudden the price of the machine went from the value of scrap metal, to $10,000. Those kinds of prices tempted some enterprising machinists to design and put on the market "mini-Pullmaxes", machines that did the same work as the original Swedish machine, but with a much smaller size, and reduced weight.

Shop Dog

Richard Kleinschmidt designed, produced, and sold a handful of these machines as well as offered plans to do-it-yourselfers. Plans are now available for free on the internet. I own a 12"(300mm) version of this well-conceived design.

Dake H100

An affordable, sturdy, mid-sized mini machine with a throat deep enough to reach into many panels. It was formerly known as the Anoka Power Hammer though in fact it is not a power hammer, but a reciprocating machine. It accepts standard 19mm square tooling.

Baileigh PH-19

The largest of the "mini-Pullmaxes", this high quality machine is a Chris Rusch design that allows the use of standard tooling.

Precision Guesswork 25

Taking up where Shop Dog left off, Andy Geelhoed of Hasting, Michigan is offering parts kits to build your own machine with a 25" (650mm) throat. That size allows for beading work anywhere on a four foot panel.

Air Hammer-Planishers

There isn't enough room in this book to discuss all the various air planishers on the market, but I do want to touch on two that are "cross-over" machines in that they are intended to be used as small power hammers, as well as air planishers.

The Precision Guesswork 25 comes as a kit and can handle 4 foot (1250mm) panels.

Kent White

Kent offers a range of hammer-planishers that are much favored by aircraft shops and fine automobile restoration facilities around the country. His machines are compact, yet powerful and meticulously tuned prior to shipment. They can be purchased with a very complete tool suite, as well as personalized lessons from Kent himself.

Baileigh MMSC-36

The MH-19 power hammer can be optioned with a very useful planishing attachment that bolts to its side to save space in a crowded shop. The new MMSC-36 shown on the next page, is a four-headed version of the attachment that when equipped with various dies become a rapid hammer shaping, and planishing station all in one.

Thumbnail Shrinking Dies

In 1919 two Finns living in Indianapolis, Otto Lindström and Toivo Mäkelä, secured a patent for what they called a "drawing-in power hammer die." We call them thumbnail shrinking dies today, but they look the same and work the same as the ones Otto and Toivo patented a hundred years ago.

Shrinking dies are brilliantly clever. As the power hammer top die goes up and down, the operator pushes in the sheet metal which when it reaches raised "thumb" of the lower die, forms into a pucker in the groove of the upper die. As the sheet is slowly pulled out and the pucker reaches over the flat part of the lower die, it is hammered down by the flat of the upper die causing it to shrink. Medieval armorers used a tucking tool to form puckers which they then hammered down on a steel plate. Shrinking dies do the same operation much more quickly and with much less physical effort.

Not much changed in the world of shrinking dies until Stan Fulton in the early 2,000s began offering plastic shrinking dies. Stan's dies are made not only with a specially engineered plastic, but by a proprietary process that leaves them extremely hard and durable. These dies are favored by coachbuilders who work in aluminum because they don't leave hammering marks which saves hours of planishing or sanding.

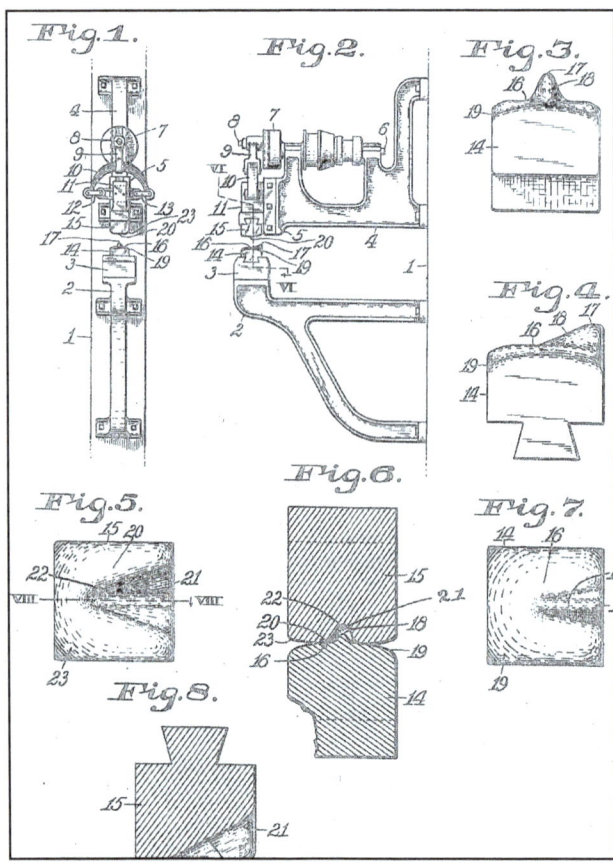

The original 1919 US Patent drawings for thumbnail shrinking dies.

Stan Fulton sells these plastic thumbnail shrinking dies which can be mounted in Pullmaxes, mini-Pullmaxes, or even Yoders and Pentingells. The plastic technology is actually a proprietary process which allows the dies to be extremely durable, yet non-marring when used on aluminum. Craig Naff has built several cars using one set, but has purchased several more sets just in case Stan stops making them!

Kent White's high quality Air Power Hammers are found in the best shops, including aero-space.

Time is money and so the latest offering from the inspired mind of tool designer Chris Rusch is this work station which will allow for rapid production in a busy shop. It is to be marketed by Baileigh and features four separate air hammers that can be fitted with a variety of tooling from shrinking, to stretching and planishing dies.

Chapter Three

'39 GMC Door

Jamie & Stella Downie

The hot rod scene is really hopping in the land of kangaroos. Like the U.S., Australia is a vast country where big American vehicles with big engines are appreciated. Unlike in the States, however, Aussies have a very limited junk pile from which to source rare parts when they're restoring or rodding out old Detroit iron, often leftovers from WWII. That's where Jamie and Stella Downie of *Kustom Garage* come in. They can make anything in metal. Hammering is a family affair and Stella is quite comfortable, and capable, around a power hammer, Pullmax, or air planisher

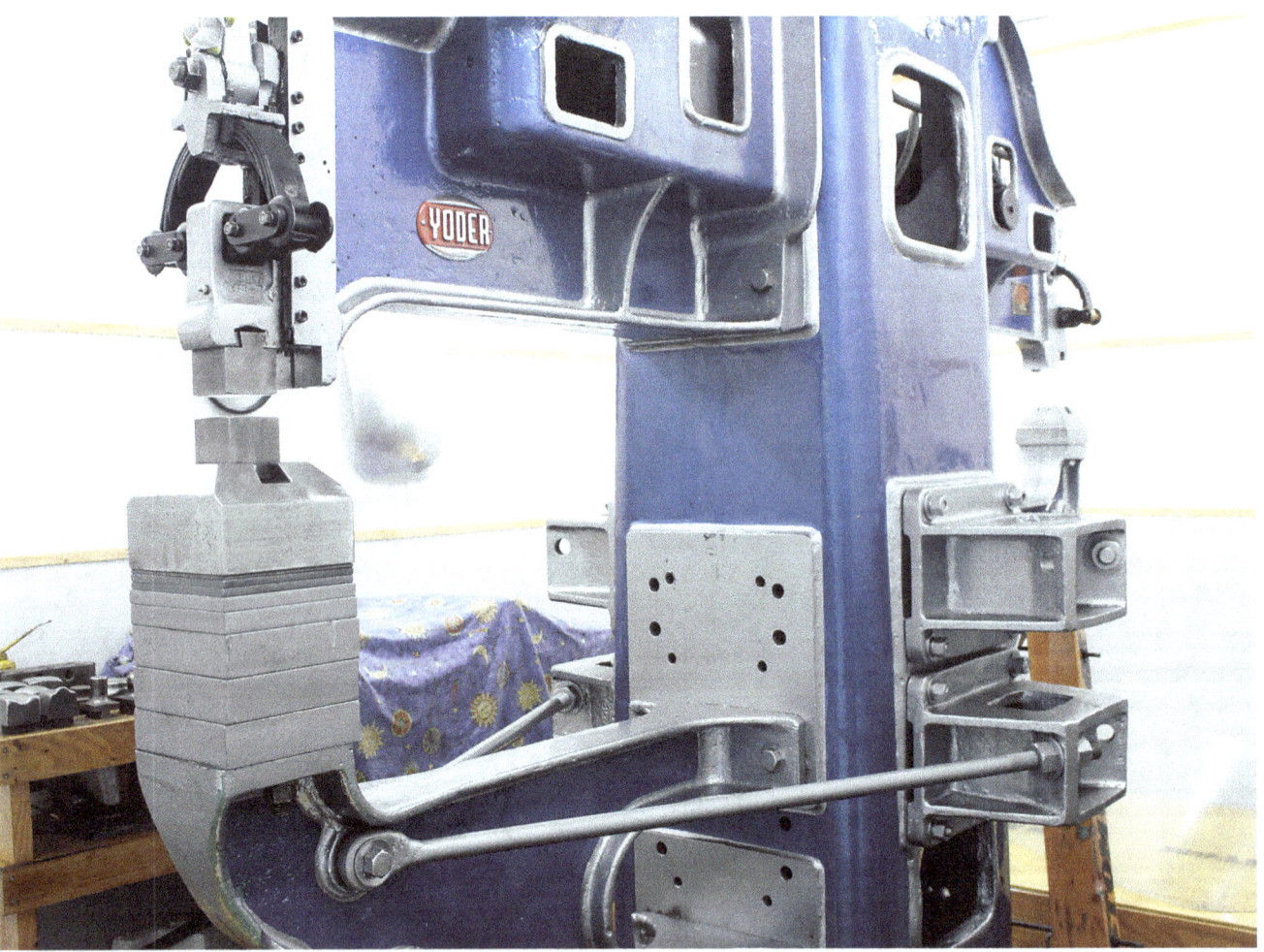

Beauty, and it's a beast! The mighty double-headed LK-90 Yoder started as an American military leave-behind from WWII, but had a K-90 arm added to it later.

Kent White's high quality Air Power Hammers are found in the best shops, including aero-space.

Time is money and so the latest offering from the inspired mind of tool designer Chris Rusch is this work station which will allow for rapid production in a busy shop. It is to be marketed by Baileigh and features four separate air hammers that can be fitted with a variety of tooling from shrinking, to stretching and planishing dies.

Chapter Three
'39 GMC Door

Jamie & Stella Downie

The hot rod scene is really hopping in the land of kangaroos. Like the U.S., Australia is a vast country where big American vehicles with big engines are appreciated. Unlike in the States, however, Aussies have a very limited junk pile from which to source rare parts when they're restoring or rodding out old Detroit iron, often leftovers from WWII. That's where Jamie and Stella Downie of *Kustom Garage* come in. They can make anything in metal. Hammering is a family affair and Stella is quite comfortable, and capable, around a power hammer, Pullmax, or air planisher

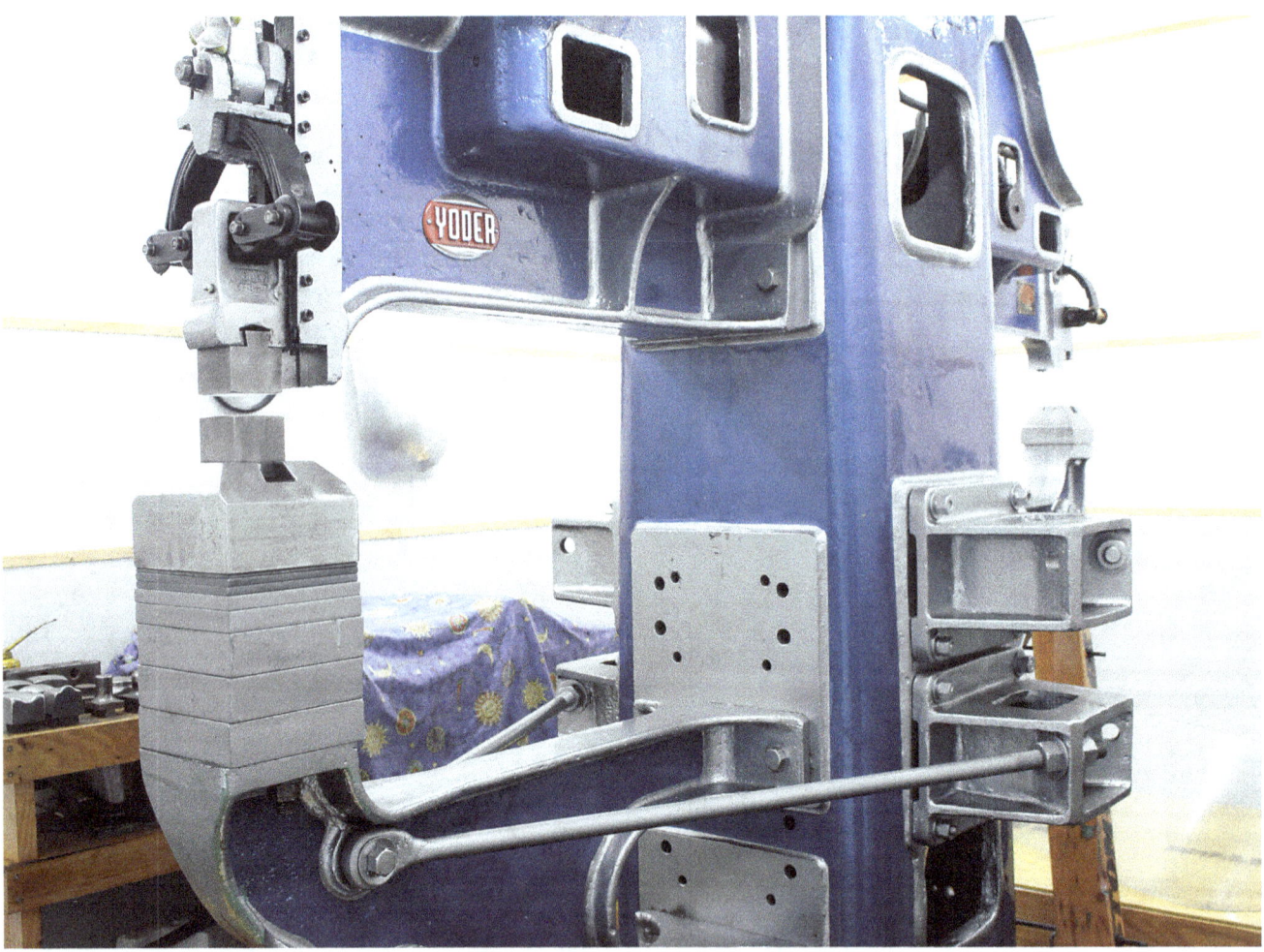

Beauty, and it's a beast! The mighty double-headed LK-90 Yoder started as an American military leave-behind from WWII, but had a K-90 arm added to it later.

Jamie cut the blank doing the final 1/4" (6mm) trim with aviation snips for accuracy.

The rusted original door had enough life left in it to make this accurate paper pattern.

*The flat **looking** door is not flat and required this buck to replicate it.*

A plastic sweep shows how much crown the panel actually has. Jamie noted where the majority of the stretching should occur for our benefit

Kustom Garage is in the Bayswater area of Melbourne, and it was there that Jamie learned traditional panel beating methods from the older generation, mostly British-trained men who used the English wheel to roll panels. After receiving a Fellowship a few years ago to study American-style metal shaping in the U.S - more use of powered machinery like power hammers and Pullmaxs - he returned home and merged the two styles.

There is a whole lot of learning in this chapter for those who study it carefully. Jamie's workmanship is nothing short of stunning.

A zinc hammer knocks the mild steel wedges into the dovetail to lock the lower die in place. Such wedges are consumables and Yoder operators will always have a tin can of spares handy.

The Yoder company still makes replacement parts for their vintage hammers, but with proper maintenance they will last a lifetime…and longer. This machine is twice as old as Jamie.

Lubricating both sides of the panel.

Jamie makes his own dies using S7 tool steel heat treated to a Rockwell 56 before they are polished.

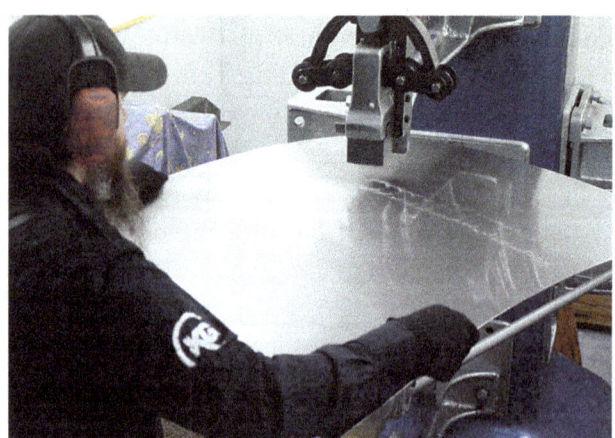

Note the rigidly precise spacing of the hammer marks. You get Jamie's precision when you plan and execute hammer blows in a consistent pattern. Hammers don't make panels, craftsmen do.

Many Yoder and Pettingell operators build raised platforms so their elbows are lower during shaping. By lowering their elbows they get better blood circulation and less fatigue.

See how Jamie's elbows are just below the plane of the lower die's top? This is the ideal level to balance ergonomics with panel control.

The only way to judge this panel is by supporting it with this buck. If it were simply placed on a flat table, it would sag in the middle and give a false indication as to its shape. (**See p.108 in Learning the English Wheel.**)

It takes many trips between the buck and the hammer to achieve the correct crown **without going past it**. Achieve your shape gradually.

Looks close except for the lift at the bottom edge. This is corrected by further crowning the panel tangentially to Jamie's hand.

Supporting a panel evenly helps prevent accidently forming the panel while shaping it. Any sagging during this stage would translate into panel twist.

The tracking marks are clearly visible in the oil film.

Note: Our 6-photo pages read down, then over and down again, as seen here. We only number the pics when the sequence might be confusing to the reader.

It is easier to check the curvature with a sweep from above, than looking under the buck. The sweep shows a flat spot under his right hand.

Gloved hands are actually more sensitive than bare hands. Jamie feels for lumps or valleys. Even the most careful operators will have them, skilled operators will have fewer of them.

The use of WD 40 creates a hydraulic barrier to stop the dies from marring the panel and makes it slide over the dies more easily, it also allows die tracking marks to be seen and followed.

Hammer low or "tight" areas to raise them.

Test fitting on the buck again. Due to space constraints, many test fits are not illustrated.

The low area is attended to through gentle bumping. A Yoder's power can be reduced by "blipping" the pedal which is connected to the motor's cone clutch. Blipping allows the clutch to slip, thus reducing power.

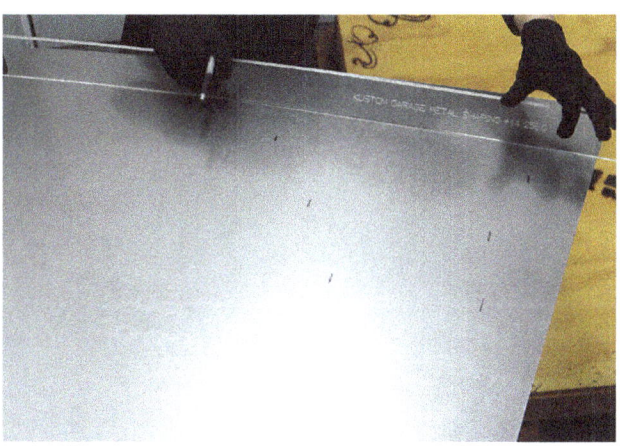

Jamie drags the sweep down the panel looking for gaps under it that indicate low spots.

Once the panel perfectly fits the buck, Jamie marks where the belt line will go.

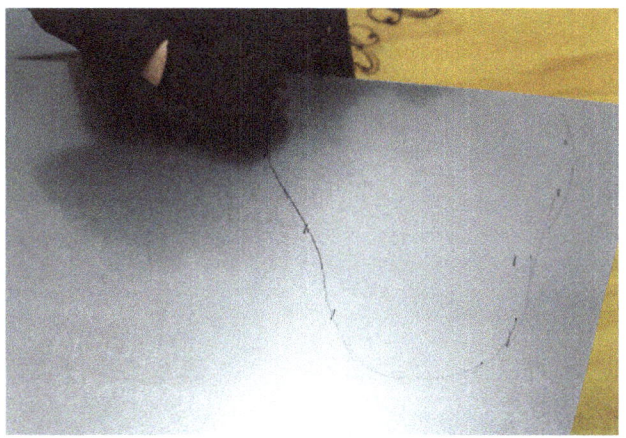

A topological map is created of those spots.

Jamie made these dies for his Pullmax. It is much easier to make flat Pullmax tooling than turn out beading dies for the same belt line on a lathe.

Stella assists guiding the panel through the Pullmax.

The last pass and the belt line is perfect.

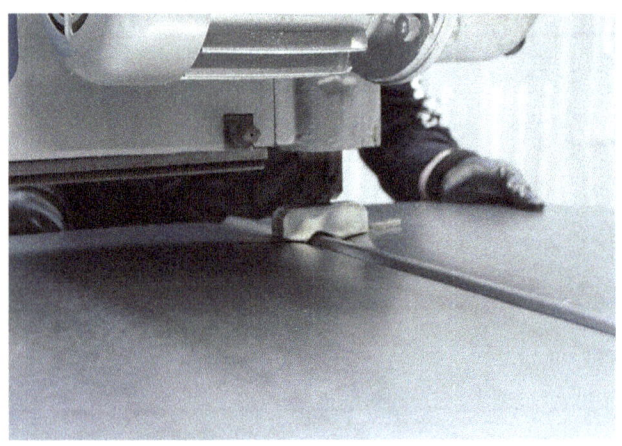
The bead is raised in a minimum of three passes. The lower die is cranked up slightly after each pass.

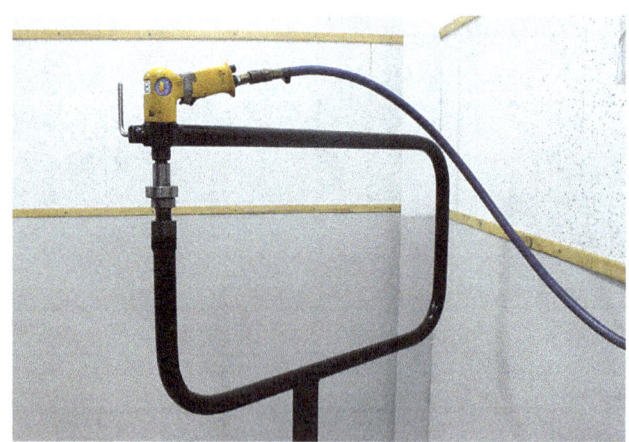
Jamie built this simple, but effective air planisher.

The deep throat depth of the Pullmax makes this job much easier. Die construction is the key to success, and you should always practice with your dies on scrap before using them on a real project. Tweaking the dies is often necessary.

The planisher tames any inconsistencies in the panel, and removes any tooling marks from the Pullmax operation.

The plywood tooling guide is smaller than the actual window and is dimensioned to guide the Pullmax tooling.

A close-up of the dies in action. Go slowly with many overlapping blows.

Window frame profile Pullmax tooling that Jamie made.

Beading the window opening caused some slight distortion which Jamie attends to with a Baileigh shrinker…

Shaping the window frame takes several passes with Stella's help. The guide has been through-bolted to the door at four corners.

…before making another pass around the guide.

The window shaping is complete. Notice the shrinking marks on the outer edge of the frame.

…and then folded by Jamie leaving…

The excess window material is trimmed away, but this rectangular section is left and will be folded over.

…this rounded profile. Note the jig required to make this simple fold.

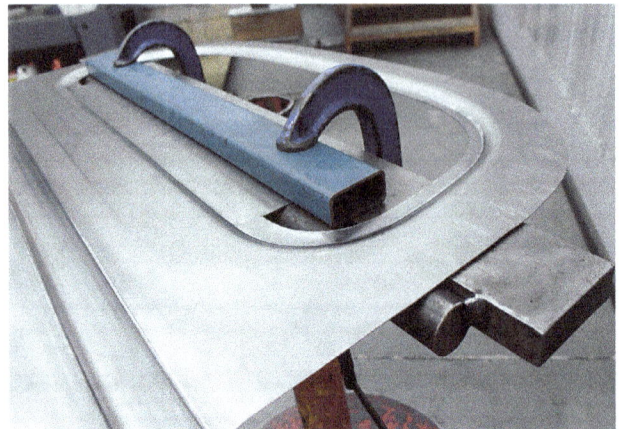

The rectangle is clamped…

Shrinking the flange to pull curvature back into the door.

Spooning out slight ripples caused by the shrinking operation.

Stretching the frame's corners.

Folding a length of steel for the inner window frame.

A perfect fit around the guide.

The guide is now used as a pattern for the frame.

Another set of Pullmax dies. These will profile the new inner frame.

Once again, several passes are required to round the frame smoothly. Oiling the steel helps during this process.

After scribing a line, he cuts away excess from the inner frame.

The rounded frame is checked against the window opening.

Tig welding the parts together. Notice the big gas lens on the torch.

Because there is a double bullnose feature around the window, precise curvature is required. Jamie uses a hammer and dolly to make everything even.

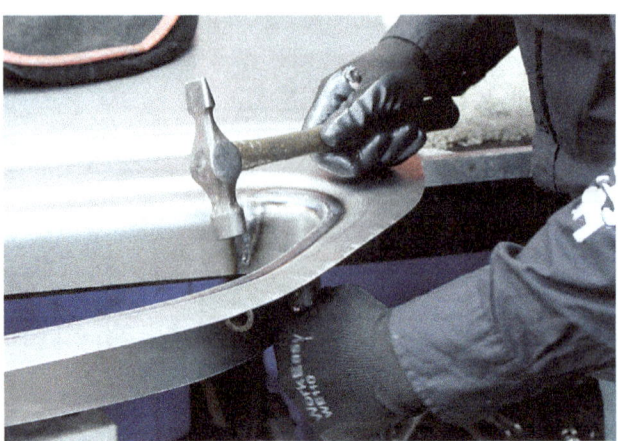

Stretching out the weld with a hammer and dolly.

Nothing more than a hand file is needed when the joint is fused correctly.

Jamie trims it away with snips. Most panel beaters only do fine cuts, ½" (13mm) or less with aviation snips.

The pattern is put back on the door to precisely locate the next operation.

Hammering flat the cut line.

A set of dividers marks the trim line on the bent over flange.

The final piece to be made goes below the window opening and will attach to the door frame itself...

...welded in place on the inner window frame.

Stella and Jamie tip the door's edges.

Only after the door is complete does he cut its final profile.

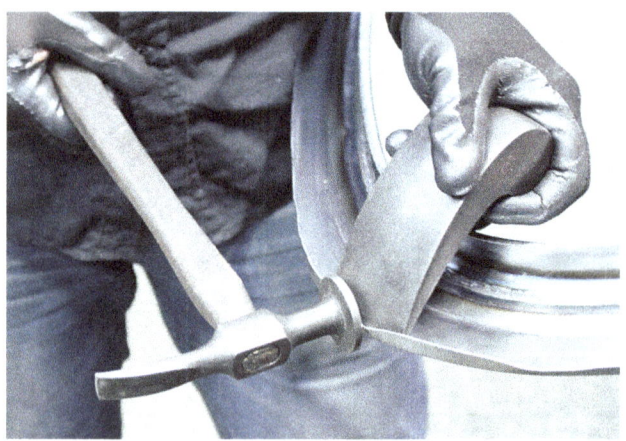
Cold shrinking the corner with a comma dolly.

Flanging die set up in the Pullmax.

Closing the flange around the door frame.

This type of precision work is typical of Kustom Garage.

Kustom Garage's Jamie and Stella Downie with their apprentices Colton and Violet. A family that hammers together stays together.

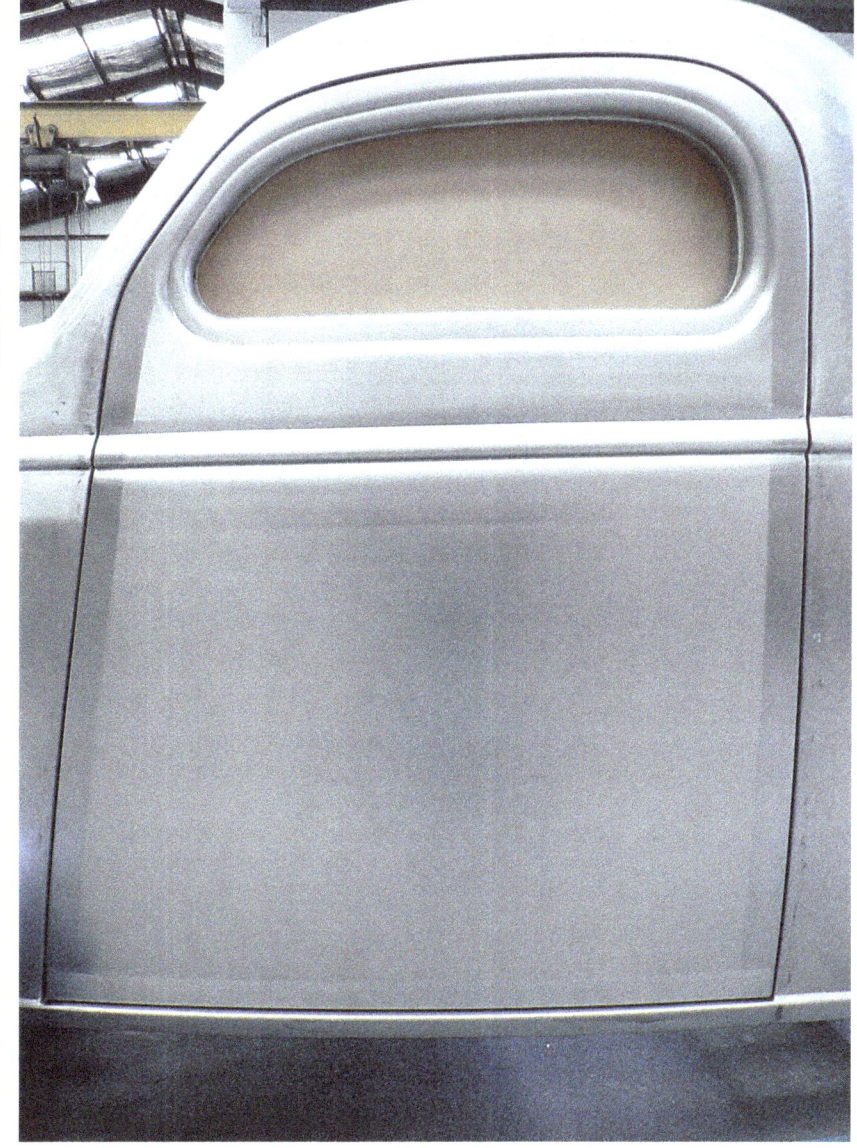

The door fitted to the cab. GMC never built a truck with door gaps this precise back in the 1930s.

Chapter Four

From Plainfield to Pebble Beach

Tommy Caruso

Tommy Caruso is truly one of the country's most talented metalshapers, yet he is also one of its most modest and self-effacing. He toils away every day in Plainfield, New Jersey making fabulous car bodies from scratch for a select clientele that includes names often found on the winner's stand at Pebble Beach. Success doesn't faze Tommy because he's already on to the next bespoke body.

Tommy got his start in his father's body shop which specialized in metal-finished repairs rather than mud and grind. One of his father's employees was an Italian immigrant who taught him to gas weld at age eleven. A few years later, inspired by Ron Fournier's book and a magazine article about Marcel Delay, he built his own English wheel which he still uses. The wheel led to power

Gabriel Voisin started out building airplanes and adapted lightweight aero construction practices to the luxury cars he built during the inter war years. Only six of these C-25 Aerodynes left his Parisian factory.

New Jersey's finest, Tommy Caruso.

Tommy built a buck that could be reconfigured for a left or right fender. The original Voisin fenders were not only not savable due to damage, but very asymmetrical.

hammers and a course with Yoder guru Fay Butler.

Renowned French car collector Peter Mullin tasked Tommy to build a new set of fenders for his exotic 1935 Voisin C-25 Aerodyne. Voisins are rarer than Bugattis and often feature fantastically styled aluminum bodies that, in the 1920 and 30s, stood them out from the rest of the luxury cars of the day. A Voisin is an event, making new fenders for them a formidable challenge. Tommy made the fenders - and the car won Pebble Beach.

Do not "guestimate" the paper pattern. An accurate pattern with a ¾" (20mm) overhang) will get you off to a good start when shaping and save you time.

Tommy puts the 3003-H14 .063 on top of a sheet of 20 gauge steel so he can use magnets to hold the pattern in place.

Panel size is limited to arm span in a one-man shop. Note the sweep rack behind Tommy.

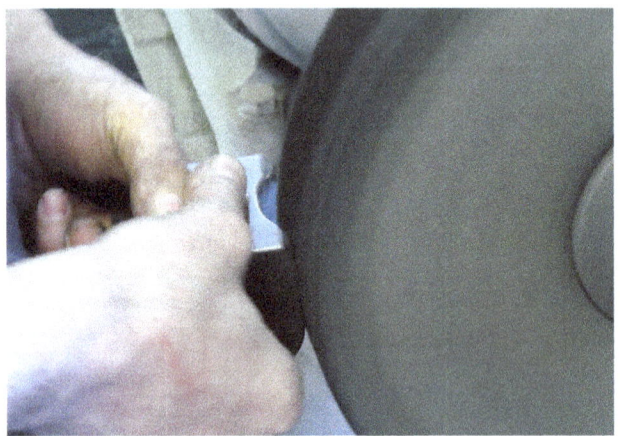

Polishing the lower shrinking die on a 5hp buffer. Dies are routinely checked for galling or scratches.

There are two lines on this panel. The solid line demarks the depth of the shrink while the dashed line is the "high light" line. Methodical planning is key to consistent curvatures.

Curling the blank before shrinking the top edge prevents a hard ridge forming - especially true when shrinking to create larger radiuses. It's important to stagger shrinks, long and short, on larger radiuses. On radiuses of 2" or less this may not be necessary.

Once the shrinks are in Tommy stretches out the panel and the curvature becomes more pronounced.

One session of shrinking was enough to work harden the panel. Tommy anneals it using an oxyacetylene flame, and soft wood. As he sweeps the flame, he pushes the stick into the panel. When it blackens, the panel has reached 750°F the annealing temp. of aluminum.

… switches over to his twin-headed Pettingell and blends the shrink line with a 24" radius die and concentrates the blows more to the ends. This raises the ends, and lowers the center. He recommends starting blends on the shrink line and moving into the panel from there.

Back in the Yoder with the shrinking dies.

The 24" radius die in action. Tommy has made many of his own dies from 3" square tool steel.

A test fit shows that there is too much arch in the edge of the panel, so Tommy …

Eight feet wide and nearly ten feet tall, the Pettingell was originally designed to save shop floor space while two operators worked. These days, solo shop owners like it because it saves having to change dies as often.

The fit is very close, and the finish actually smoother than it may appear.

Access through a buck is critical to check panel fit. The top needs to come over some more.

Hammering just inboard of the edge takes the waviness out of the edge. (See LEARNING the ENGLISH WHEEL to understand how this works.)

Tommy blends both sides of the highlight line together through carefully planned rows of hammer blows. Sweeping a panel through a hammer randomly only creates waves and divots.

Flattening the panel laterally further pulls over the edge. You must anticipate this.

Even closer now...

1) …so back to the 24" die for some more stretching.

2) There are few absolutely flat panels in coachbuilding. Even the slab side of the Voisin fender has a very slight crown so as to avoid "oil canning" as the car moves. Tommy is putting a touch of crown into the vertical side of the fender.

4) After an hour's work the panel is down to nit-picking. Note the row of Aston-Martin DBs awaiting Tommy's attention.

3) While working, a bolt under the tool holder worked loose so Tommy retightens it with a hex wrench.

5) The bottom edge of the panel is slightly crowned.

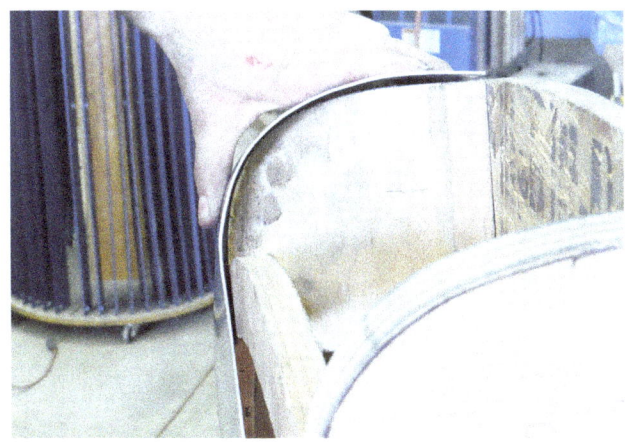

Excellent fit to a buck station. Tommy recommends all panel joints be over a buck station as it is a repeatable location during test fits, and more exact than a theoretical point in space.

Tommy built this planisher up from plate and tubing, grinding the corners and body filling it so it would look like it was cast.

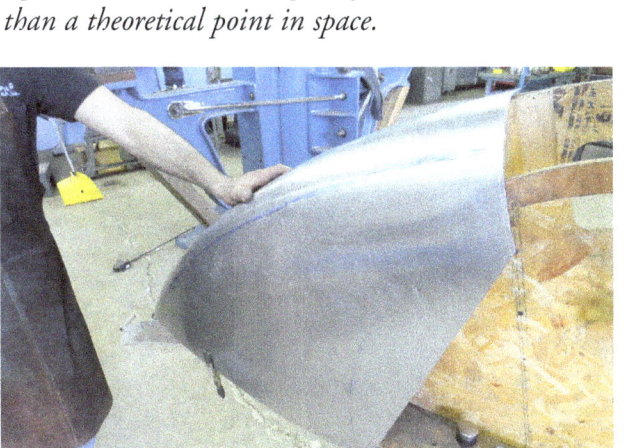

Notice how the highlight line is exactly where he planned it would be.

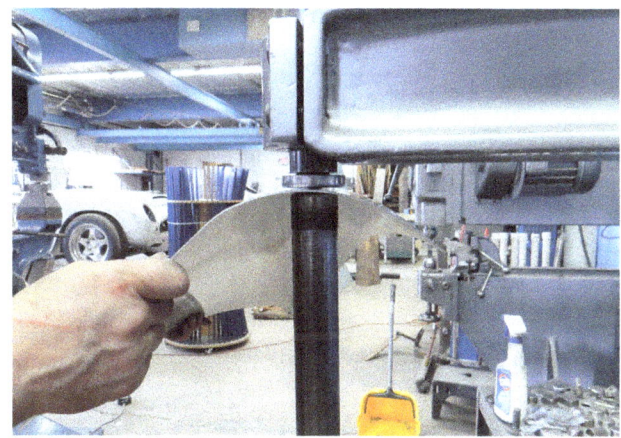

The bottom anvil should always be as close in radius, to the part being planished, as possible.

Whether using a power hammer, or an air planisher, the panel should be lubricated with oil first.

It is good practice to pre-plan that the planish will add a little more crown to the final panel. Coachbuilding is like playing chess player, winners think several steps ahead.

The front panel for the outside repeated the same steps for the rear panel. Here Tommy lays out the pattern for the inner rear panel.

Using a short sweep he establishes a "fair" line for the valley between the wheel arch and the flange.

He uses a razor to nick the paper so he can mark interior areas with a Sharpie. He tries not to scratch or nick aluminum panels to avoid stress risers. As a licensed pilot, Tommy is aware of the dangers of stress risers on an aluminum skin.

He extends the faired line with the aid of some welding rod to the front paper pattern.

The paper pattern for the inner rear panel. Note how Tommy only wants a small flange turned to join the other rear panel. It is not recommended to plan panel joints inside a "valley".

With the blank cut and marked, he runs the flange line through his Pullmax to create just a slight indentation. This line will thin the metal just enough to later help define the valley's bottom.

The cylinder to the right acts as a depth control as the panel passes through the Pullmax.

…it will only take a few light blows from the 36" radius die to blend the shrinks into the panel smoothly.

Flipping the panel around, Tommy shrinks the top on one of his Yoders.

Power hammers can do very fine work and leave a paintable finish as this photo illustrates.

Once again the depth of the shrinks fall exactly on the line as planned, and because the panel was curled during the process…

A cardboard "outside" template is cut so…

...he can more accurately monitor the position of the valley and crowns.

Hammer blows should slightly overlap and be evenly spaced. A power hammer doesn't make the part, the operator does. All stages must be pre-planned and carefully controlled.

Tommy creates the valley with simple hand tools, a T-dolly and wood mallet.

Just as with an English wheel, when forming reverses you work inverted and sweep your arms upward.

The flange is stretched inverted because it is a reverse curve.

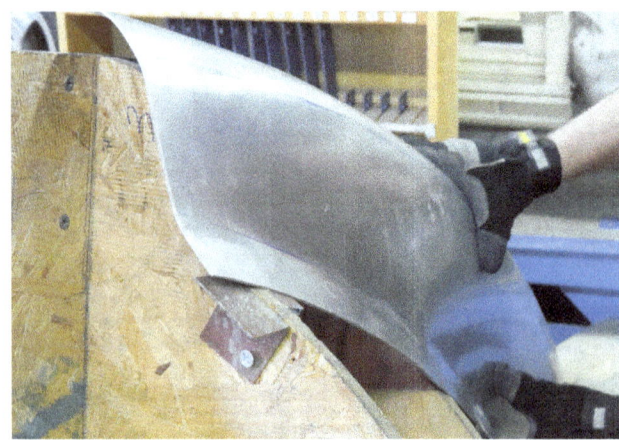

A test fit shows the top edge needs to come over more.

Tommy returns to the Yoder and increases the crown using a 12" radius lower die.

Another round of shrinking the top edge, blending it, and redefining the valley is required to settle the panel.

While using a highly radiused die he maintains his distance from the highlight line. Note the 3-phase wiring to the machine.

About six hours into the process, Tommy has moved on to the front upper panel. The top has been shrunk, the initial valley formed.

The top has come down and the fit is close…

Although the top edge it's close, Tommy points to where the valley has slid out from the buck.

He marks a new valley line about an inch (26mm) above his initial position.

He forms the new valley on a T-dolly…

…and checks it again.

Satisfied with its placement, he further defines it using a home-made bar slapper and a sandbag.

The fit is 99% there, and it only needs final planishing.

The inner front panel is almost entirely crown except for this one area he points to.

No hammering yet, just a prefold. Marked lines creates a "map" to help Tommy visualize where hammering needs to happen.

Tommy pushes down on the front and back of the panel so it doesn't dance between the die. Such dancing causes random blow patterns which lead to an uneven panel.

A permanent fold is introduced to the panel on thus tubular bender with a bar welded along its top. A slight gap under the bar allows the sheet metal to be slipped in.

After only a few minutes the panel is taking shape. It is very easy to over-stretch a panel like this and create a lump, so go slowly and test fit often.

A 36" radius die and intermittent "blip" steps on the pedal allow the Pettingell to strike the panel with the moderate blows necessary to create the mild crown.

Because this panel makes a sudden transition under Tommy's finger, he has drawn a line to precisely locate it to the buck during each test fitting.

The amount of space under the flattened panel shows how much crown had to be created. To repeat, there are very few truly flat panels in coachbuilding.

Then he trims away the excess.

Tommy makes the flange line. This panel took less than thirty minutes to form.

Using a rare Erco Former, he easily creates a flange with a few passes through the machine.

He accurately locates a second line ¾" (20mm) outboard of the first line.

A mallet and Pexto stake flatten waves in the flange.

The flange is tightened where required in an Erco kick shrinker.

Linear dies can get close to edges. Be careful not to over stretch when using these!

To use a John Glover term, it has a "vacuum fit" to the buck!

A stand mounted hand-held planisher tweaks the other panels.

Planishing in Tommy's home-made CP inspired machine.

Panels are test fitted together for approval.

Inner panels are then attached to the buck.

Tommy oxyacetylene welds them together using parent metal from cut off scraps.

So are the outer panels.

The final piece necessary to finish the fender is a trim molding that follows the wheel opening. It begins as a 1 ½" (37mm) piece of flat aluminum bent in the brake.

When all are in position, they are scribed and trimmed.

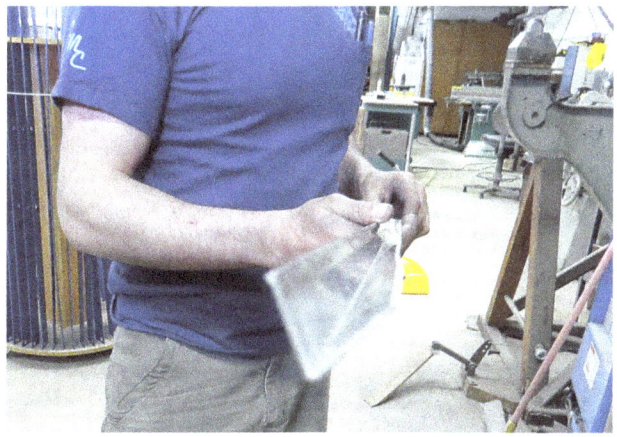

The "V" section is…

...oiled, and fed through specially shaped dies in the Pullmax to curve one of the legs. Several passes are used so as not to crack the aluminum.

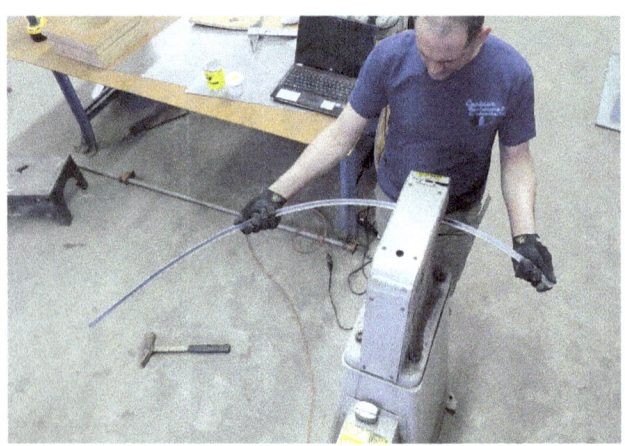

Another round of shrinking tightens it further.

The Erco shrinker brings the molding around to the proper curvature.

Finally, a pass through special dies on a rotary machine erases any waviness and tooling marks.

Shrinking one leg causes the molding to warp, so Tommy flattens it back down.

A close-up of the dies Tommy machined.

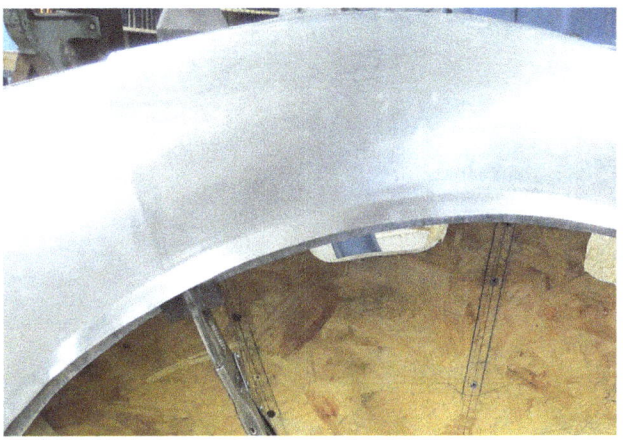

The trim fits just as Gabriel Voisin intended it to.

The finished C-25 Aerodyne with the unusually braced fenders.

Tommy's Top 12 Tips:

1. Always over-shrink a little and then planish back to fit the buck.
2. Try to avoid two highlight lines on one panel. If unavoidable, they should be as distant from each other as possible.
3. Don't weld in a valley if you can avoid it because it's very hard to metal finish there.
4. Mark buck station points on the panel, and always mark accurately.
5. Join panels at buck station points for welding. If necessary, make an extra station in the buck.
6. Check for galling or scratches on dies, especially when working aluminum.
7. A panel will "sing" to you when it is close to being the proper shape.
8. Don't cut out wheel arches and large openings until the panel is nearly finished. The panel becomes too floppy.
9. When blending a shrink ridge, work from the ridge down into the panel.
10. On reverse curves it is better to start the curve with linear stretch dies and finish with radius dies.
11. Polish dies when you feel them dragging. Don't depend just on oil.

Tommy Caruso with the crew from Stone Barn Auto Restorations stand with the car's owner, Peter Mullin, after winning first place at the Pebble Beach Concours d'Elegance. Wow!

Chapter Five

Three Machines, One Perfect Part

Craig Naff

The Swiss company W. Eckold AG builds a legendary line of power shaping tools that fall somewhere between a power hammer and a reciprocating machine. Their most popular feature is that they can reach deeply into a panel and shrink, or stretch using beautifully designed and crafted proprietary dies. Panel shapers lucky enough to have a variety of powered machinery will take advantage of each one's attributes. The Eckold offers finesse, the Pullmax simplicity, and the Yoder, power.

Like Eckold, Craig Naff has a legendary reputation for quality. This southern gentleman got into metalshaping because a high school shop

Not many Model A Phaetons were produced. The phaeton body style was usually associated with well-heeled chauffeur driven swells of the 1930s, not the masses, Ford's usual clientele.

teacher noticed his potential and taught him the rare skill of precision gas welding as well as the rudiments of hammer and dolly work. Those skills were enough to get Craig a job at prestigious White Post Restorations a few miles up the road near Winchester, Virginia at age 19. Within months he was their lead metal man. Four years later he had his own metal shop, but was soon enticed by Boyd Coddington to relocate to California.

After building many hot rods for notable celebrities, including the famous Cadzilla for ZZ Top, he returned to his native Shenandoah Valley where he opened a shop. Customers from across the nation now seek him out whether to build a hot rod, or rebuild a Ferrari. His workmanship is utterly flawless.

In this sequence Craig builds a rear apron for a rare 1930 Ford Model A Phaeton. Very simple appearing, low crown panels are often the hardest to make and fit. It took Craig four days to create the buck, tooling, and the panel itself.

Master panel beater, Craig Naff

The car's owner was able to source a copy of the original blueprints for the apron. How many times do you get that lucky!?

Craig used the plans to make this buck out of MDF (medium density fiberboard).

The much coveted Eckold Piccolo. Contrary to what some believe, it will not make panels for you! You've still got to have the skill, and the big wallet to afford one.

All good panels start with a carefully marked, and cut, pattern.

The Eckold Piccolo is fitted with dies made from plastic deck material. 12 foot (3.7 meters) boards of the decking are about $25 and can make dozens of dies strong enough to shape steel.

Proof that plastic dies can move steel. This is a forming operation rather than a shaping one..

A flange is tipped into the lower edge and then stretched under where the clamps are using linear stretch dies in the Yoder to curve the panel.

Craig made these dies some years before in steel, and uses them now in his Pullmax.

The flange is run through the Pullmax in several passes. After each pass, Craig decreases the gap between the dies. A test fit on the buck shows a perfect fit. Notice how the apron is actually a subtle reverse curve.

The bottom band of the apron is formed as a second piece in the Pullmax and is then welded to the main panel.

An utterly perfect weld requiring little finish work.

Another set of Pullmax dies will fine tune the shape of the welded joint..

Welding will always shrink a joint somewhat. A gentle pass through the dies will stretch it back into shape.

These mounting recesses were created using…(INSET) …this stamp set machined by Craig.

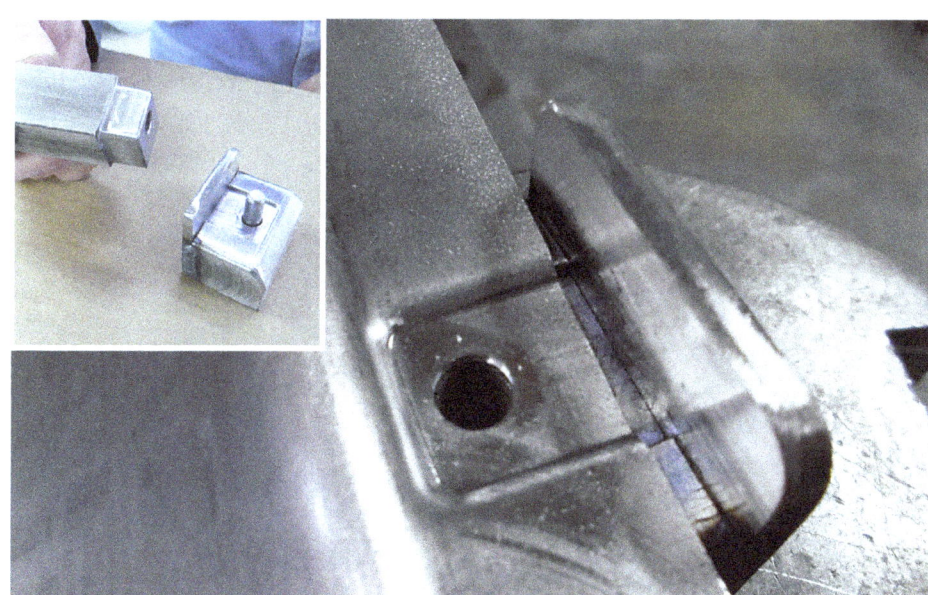

Compare the finished piece to the blueprints. Even Henry Ford couldn't tell an original from Craig's work!

Chapter Six

The Academy for the Art of Metal Shaping

Finally, A College for Coachbuilders!

There used to be a time when shop classes were taught all across the country. Classes where students were exposed to woodworking and simple metal craft. But these days a splinter in a young scholar's finger could lead to a lawsuit, and who has time for sheet metal when work sheets are waiting that might help a child score higher on a standardized test?

The fact is, manual arts have been maligned for decades by the education industry which has

*Students at the **Academy for the Art of Metal Shaping** learn their trade while working on some of the world's most exotic cars.*

62

pushed expensive, and for them, profitable, liberal arts education. Is it any wonder America, and other western nations, now have a serious shortage of skilled craftsmen?

The dramatic rise in the value of collector cars recently has exposed the fact that there aren't enough people who know how to build new bodies for rare cars. Who knows how to build anything anymore, especially one-off metal car bodies?

Mark Gerisch has come forward with a long overdue solution to this problem and has started a school for metal shapers. His *Academy for the Art of Metal Shaping (AAMS)* is a non-profit 501 (c) (3) educational institution located in Green Bay, Wisconsin with the sole mission to turn out capable, and *certified* coachbuilders. Mark wants to establish recognized standards of workmanship and competencies in a craft that has not had them before in America. Overseas, and especially in Britain, panel beating was a recognized skill and guilds and governmental councils oversaw the training and certification of students. Typically, a student left school at age 14, entered into a formal apprentice program, and earned his or her competencies while on the job at a real factory or workshop. Mark wants to bring some of that style of training to America, and so as part of the *Academy's* curriculum students from their first year

Andrew Pierce and Chris Herber use a sweep to gauge the profile of an Abarth 850 racer car.

Mark Gerisch works with Mike Wagner on a reverse curve for a 1925 Miller Indy car.

63

Seat time in a classroom is not common in this very "hands on" institution.

are required to undertake a work-study program with an established business, usually a restoration shop.

In the *Academy* Mark starts students off with a sandbag and mallet, and works them up in stages to an English wheel and then the power hammer. Welding, planishing, annealing, lofting, and many other skills are taught along the way, including the fundamentals of business management. Most of Mark's students anticipate owning their own shop one day.

The formal Masters Course lasts two years. This is the the complete course on coachbuilding. But AAMS also offers two and five day courses, and an extended course.

As the program has grown, it has partnered with businesses and other schools. The *AAMS* recently established an off-campus site at *Road America* in Elkhart Lake, Wisconsin.

If splinters don't frighten you and sheet metal shaping is in your blood, Mark Gerisch's *Academy for the Art of Metal Shaping* may be the right fit for you and your future.

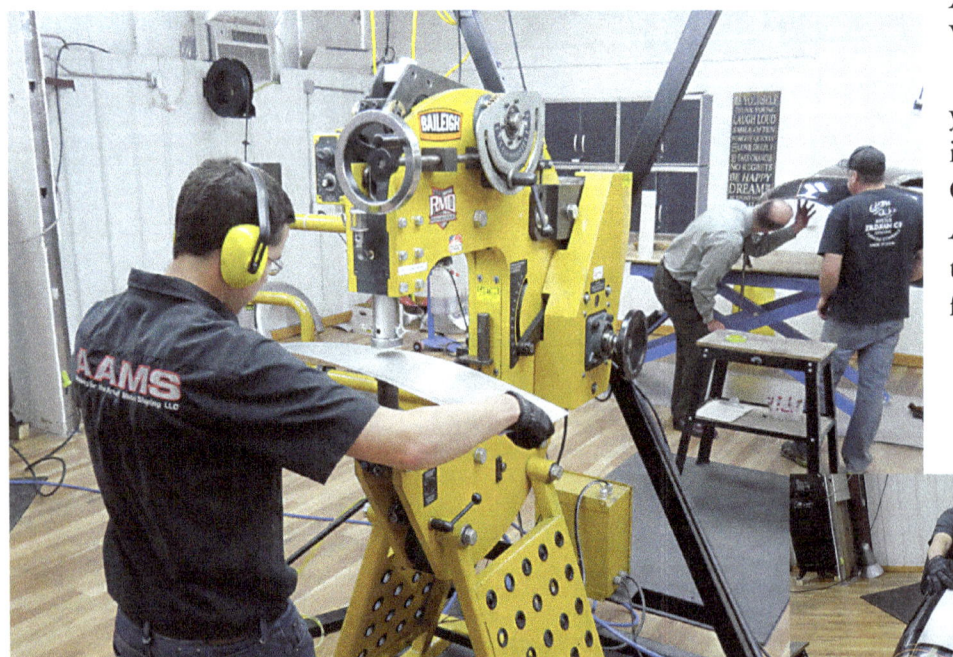

Andrew works on the boot valley for a 427 Cobra, note the test fit.

Welding instruction includes oxy-acetylene…

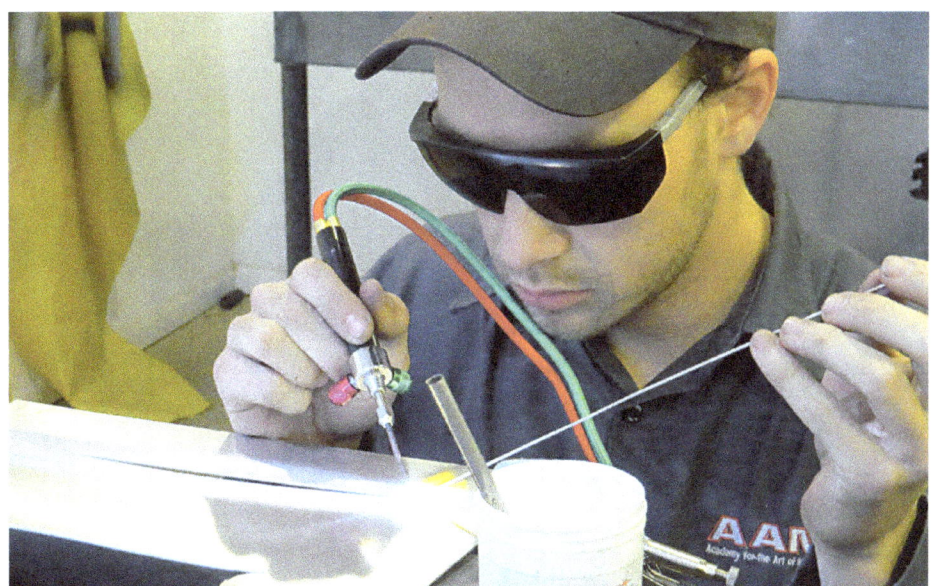

…MIG…

…and TIG.

Here Andrew fits a wire buck to a custom Miata panel.

Motorcycle tins created by Chris.

*Mark Naglich owns Lakeside Rod and Custom in Washington state. He came to the **Academy** to learn power hammer skills.*

Mark instructs Chris on how to pattern a Ferrari 250 GTO bonnet.

Dan Vice uses a body file to finish a weld on the Abarth's new fender.

Mike Wagner locates the center of the cowl he wheeled for the Miller.

Chapter Seven - Part One

AAMS Students

Speed Build a Ferrari 250 GTO

During my visit to the *Academy for the Art of Metal Shaping* Mark Gerisch invited back some former students to work with current students and guest instructors to speed build the nose of a Ferrari 250 GTO on a Saturday and Sunday. The idea was to showcase how much his students had learned after only their first trimester in the two year Master Course program. The action was fast, furious, and productive. After the two day speed build the students themselves took over the project and over the course of the next week of classes finished the other nose panels. I don't remember having this much fun in class when I was in school!

Lower Cheek Panel - Andrew Pierce worked with guest instructor Dave Byron to shape the highly crowned under cheek which fits below the headlight. Dave believes that proper planning, and accurately laying out a hammering pattern on the panel are the keys to success on a power hammer.

Andrew and Dave examine the Ferrari and consider their shaping options. It's a classic crown shape which means shrink the edges and raise the center.

Laying out panels for both sides of the car saves time in the long run.

They use low-tack tape to adhere the pattern paper to the extremely valuable car.

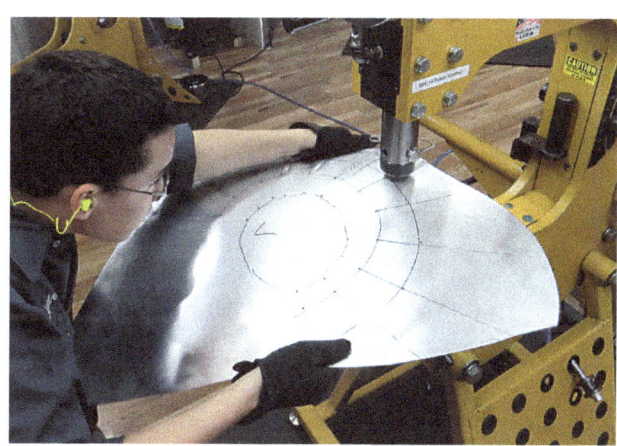

Andrew carefully tracks down the radial lines as he shrinks in the MH-19.

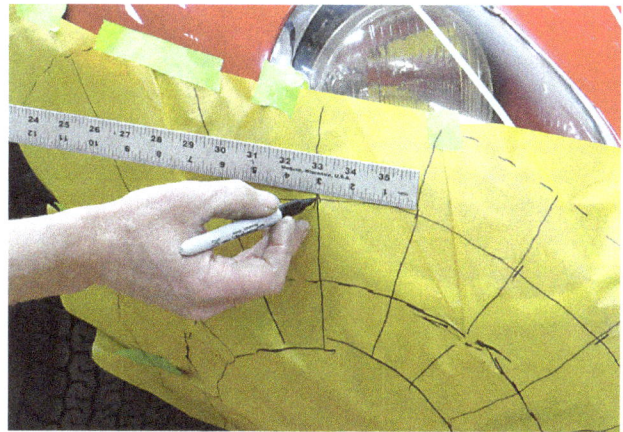

Dave believes in always measuring with a ruler as you lay out shrinking lines on a pattern. Uneven lines lead to uneven panels which just take more work to fix. Less haste, more speed.

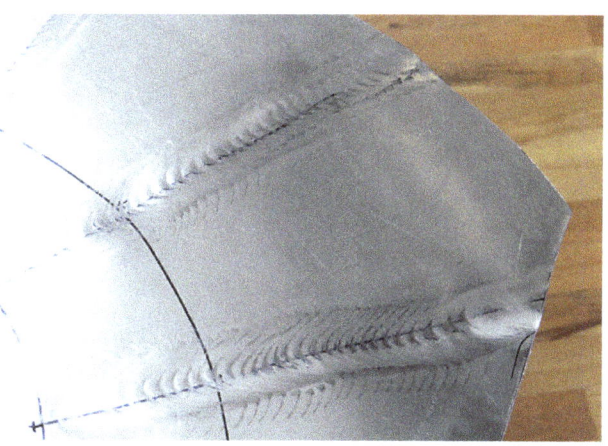

This type of consistency leads to a good final panel.

Dave assesses the progress. Much more shrinking will be needed.

The second test fit shows major improvement. You can just see a chrome side-marker lamp near Dave's left hand that is keeping the panel off the car.

Andrew goes back to work. Notice the LED light bar attached to the hammer's frame.

As Andrew shrinks, he pulls down slightly on the panel to form it.

Once the panel begins to settle on the car, trim away most of the excess.

The MH-19's final hammer speed is controlled by a foot pedal. Step harder, the hammer hits harder. Legacy machines have cone clutches which make it difficult to "feather" the hammer.

Initial speed control is through this dial. Variable Frequency Drive (VFD) motors on the new power hammers are a significant improvement over the old cone-clutch system.

A contour gauge finds the radius…

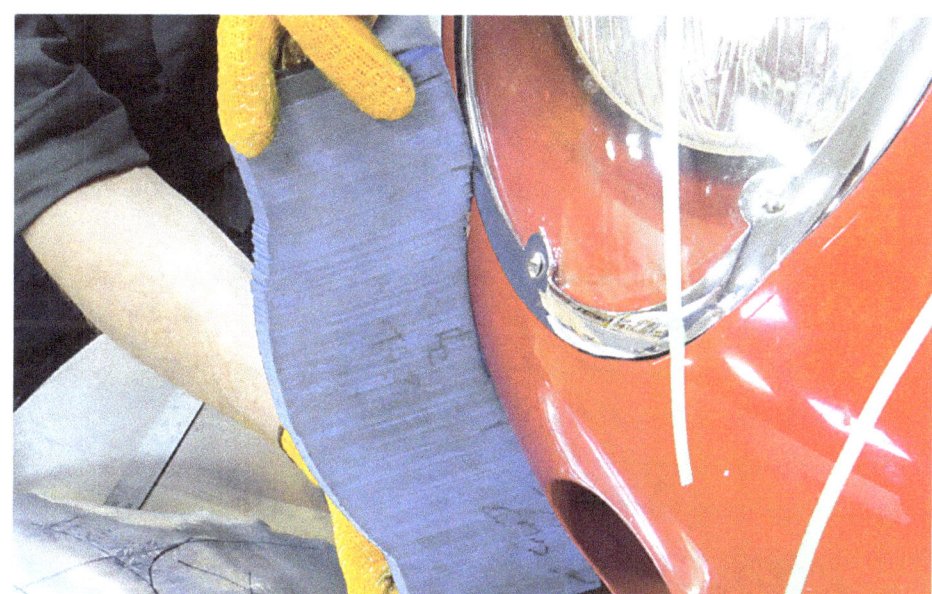

…in order to select the correct radius die to blend the shrinks.

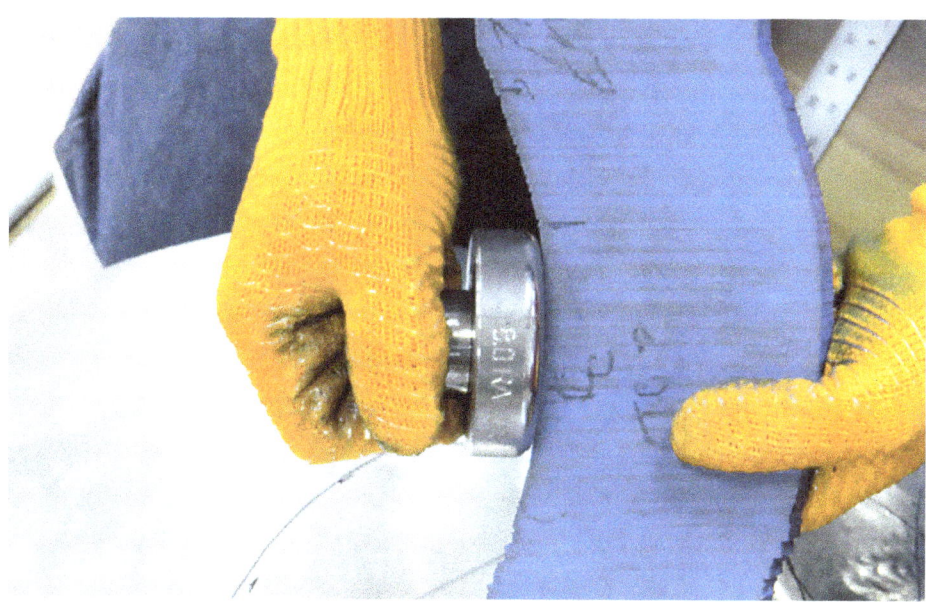

Andrew blends the shrinks back into the center of the panel. He has decreased the power of the hammer now that he is no longer shrinking.

The side marker lamp made it impossible to accurately gauge the panel as it nears completion, so he takes it over to the CNC milled MDF (medium density fiberboard) buck.

The MH-19 can be set to a very light planishing stroke which Andrew uses to smooth the panel.

Light lines without waviness are an excellent way to assess your panel.

Mark casts a critical eye and points out some areas that need attention.

Andrew address some final issues by lightly planishing them.

He uses the shear to trim the headlight bucket opening.

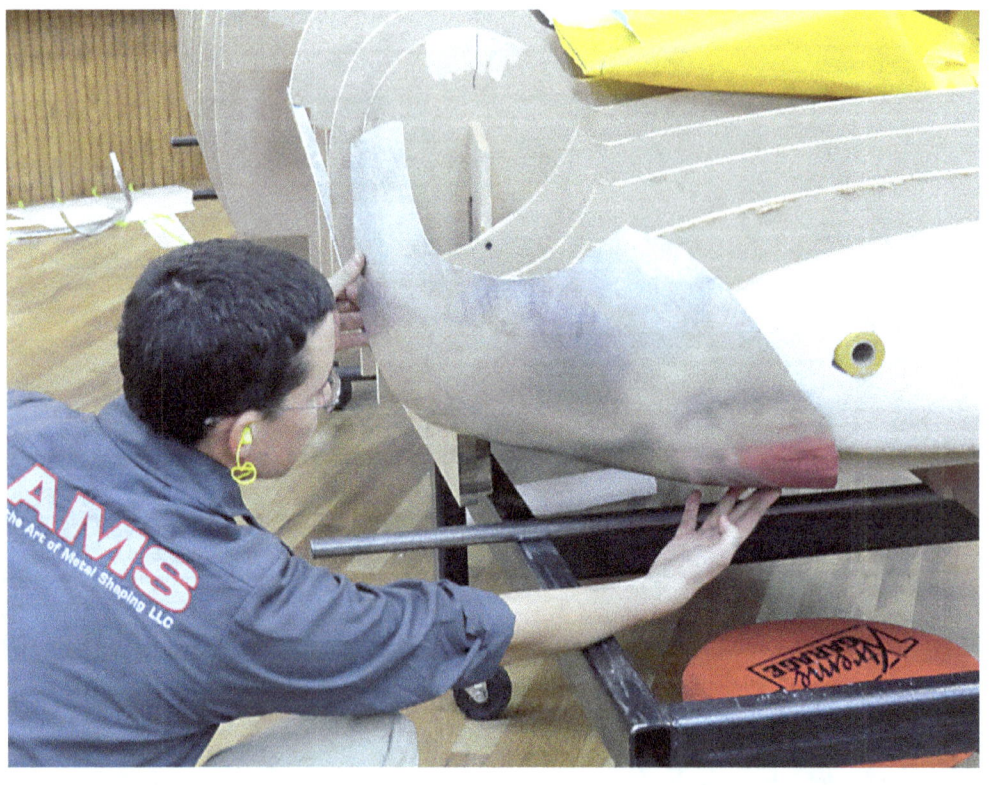

As you can see, after all that work, the panel fits well and has a good finish.

Chapter Seven - Part Two

AAMS Students Upper Fender

Dan Vice was given the job of building the outer fender panels. Shrinking along the top edge was the major shaping requirement. Once the top was shrunk and blended, it was a matter of forming the top portion of the front fender with the help of the E-wheel equipped with the rubber upper wheel.

Mark and Dan lay out the paper pattern. Ruffles along the top indicate shrinks are necessary.

Dan cut out the wheel arch. Some shapers will leave in the wheel opening material until after the shaping is done so the panel is not floppy. Note the shrink lines on the upper edge.

Dan supports the panel with his lower arm and pulls down with his fingertips. Panels must not "dance" between the dies.

Curling the panel while shrinking helps the shrinking process. Dan is using the new Baileigh MH-37HD for the first time.

Once the shrinks are in, Mark joins Dave to blend them into the panel using radius dies.

He alternates long shrinks with short ones. Note the machine's speed controls.

Mark assesses the finish and calls for a bit more blending...

1) …which they work on together.

3) The apex is formed in the English wheel using a rubber upper wheel, and a highly radiused anvil.

2) The apex of what will be the crown is marked on the panel.

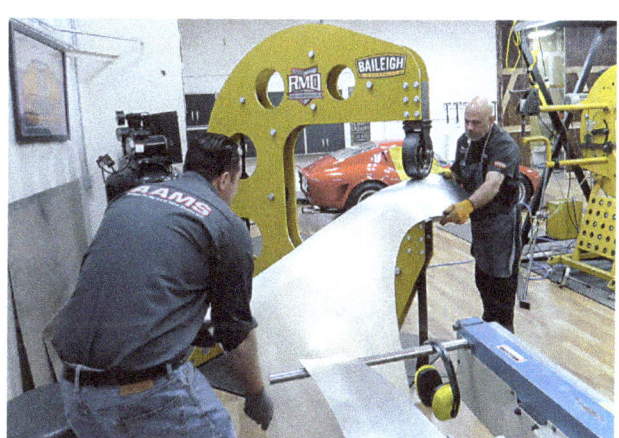

4) This operation does not change the shape (area) of the panel, it changes the form (arrangement).

5) The panel is ready for trimming and flanging.

Chapter Seven - Part Three
AAMS Students Fender Reverse

Austin Paruch, the lead panel crafter for *Motion Products*, the nation's foremost builder of Ferrari bodies, served as a guest instructor and guided Chris Herber to create the most difficult panel on the car, the reverse between the wheel arch and the hood.

Austin measures the reverse "valley" on the buck.

Chris and Austin create the pattern. Austin likes to note on the pattern where each station of the buck is located.

Chris uses the rubber upper wheel and a moderately crowned lower anvil, to place an impression along the marked valley.

Chris prepares the blank. Long panels like this are difficult to work with until they have shape and stiffness in them.

The technique of using a rubber upper wheel to creat this line, will actually form a valley without stretching the panel.

Austin points to the curved line that forms the "valley".

The crown above the wheel is created by stretching in the MH-37HD.

In less than a minute the wheel arch is beginning to rise.

Chris works the panel back and forth in evenly spaced rows. Power hammering is not random hammering.

A radius stretch die.

A linear stretch die.

The effect of a radius die is a lot like dropping a pebble in a pond.

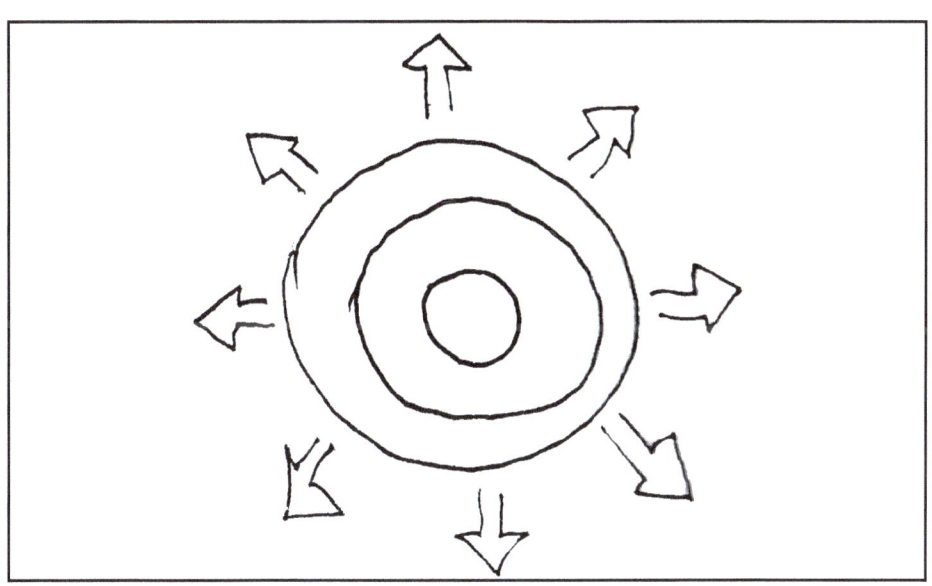

As the lineal die moves in a straight line, it splays the metal out on either side.

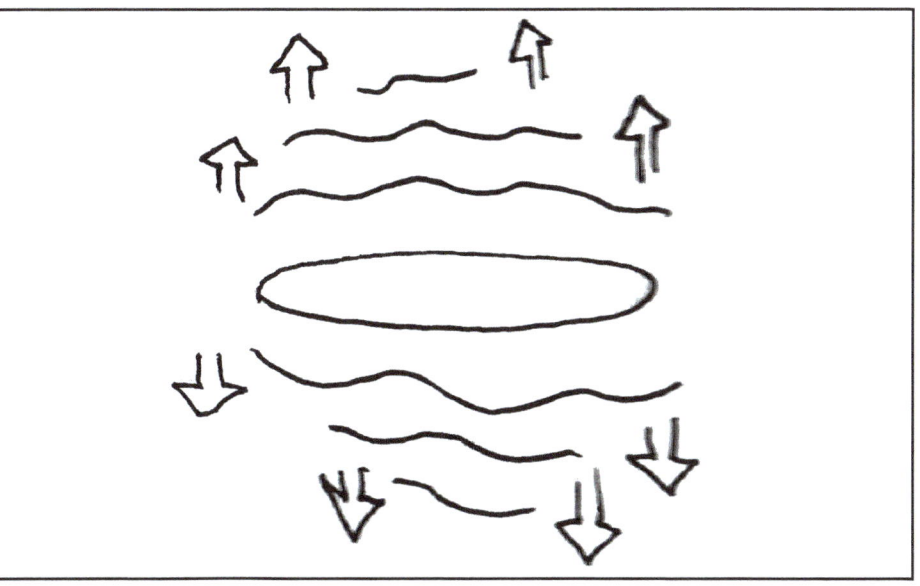

Using a linear stretch die on the edge of the hood side brings the panel around, thus creating a reverse.

The panel has come down at the nose, and up over the wheel. The valley appeared just where it was planned.

Austin marks some "tight" areas for Chris to stretch.

The panel is rocking somewhat on the middle buck station so it needs some raising there.

Chris chooses to wheel the tight areas out using light pressure. This will blend the different panel zones as well as relieve any stress in it.

Because it has been worked so much, Chris decides to anneal the panel to make it softer and easier to shape.

After wheeling, the panel is test fitted once again.

Chris is satisfied with the fit.

Chapter Seven - Part Four

AAMS Students
Lower cheek fabrication using rubber die

In the Academy students learn not just how to shape panels, but how to shape them more quickly because one day their pay will be directly tied to their ability to produce. In this sequence Mark shows Mark Naglich how a crowned panel can be raised very quickly using an upper die made from high durometer rubber. The technique is great for things like hood scoops, or blisters, but Mark cautions that you must stay away from edges of the panel when using it or the panel will shrink in. A moment's inattention could cause the surrounding areas to deform very quickly.

Mark Naglich learns how to crown quickly using a rubber upper die. The cheek piece took shape in a few minutes.

Planishing with the flat top die.

The whole process took less than fifteen minutes.

Mark carefully overlaps the blows and the "bag of walnuts" disappears.

Note the smooth finish, and the good fit.

Chapter Seven - Part Five

AAMS Students Ferrari Cowl

Andrew makes the cowl piece under the guidance of Mark with Chris assisting. Though much of this work is done with the power hammer, the English Wheel, equipped with a rubber upper wheel, makes the job of pulling a panel in tighter, with form, much easier.

The cowl blank in position. Inboard of the wheel arches the panel must dive down and then immediately rise towards the center of the car. This requires a wide reverse.

Using linear stretch dies in the power hammer, Andrew forms the cowl's flange that goes up towards the windshield.

First test fit. The left and right sides need to go down, so…

The long panel requires help, but in little more than a minute the flange is formed.

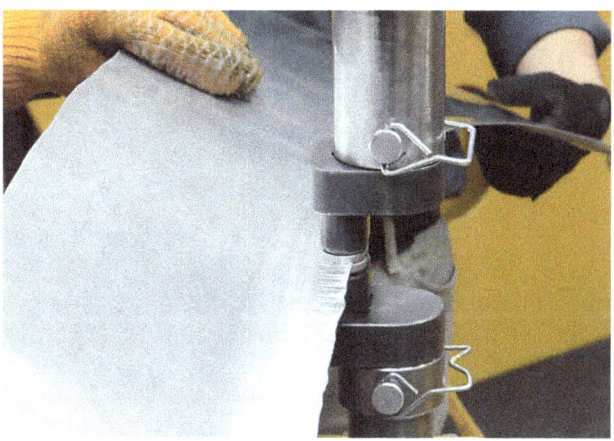

…using the stretching jaws in the MH-19 Andrews spreads the flange on each end. Equipped with these jaws, the machine becomes a power stretcher, or shrinker.

The intersection between the flange and the cowl is a rounded valley which is formed using the rubber upper wheel in the English wheel.

The flange has a slight arch in it which matches the contour of the buck.

1) The central area of the cowl is very slightly crowned with a 36" radius die. Note the red LED BPM (beats per minute) gauge on the MH-37-HD.

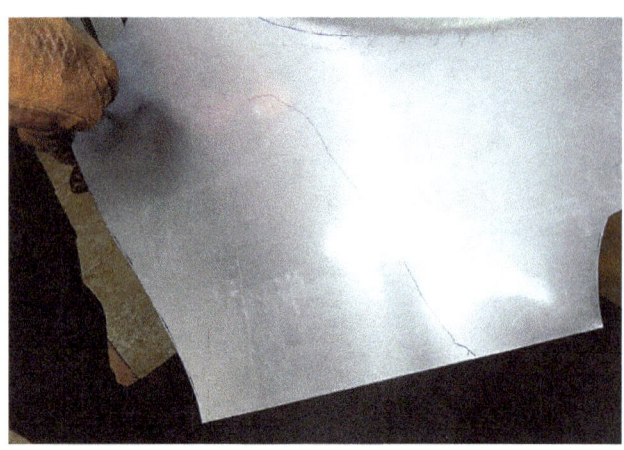

3) The ends of the panel must roll over the sides, but there is also a reverse inboard of the line Andrew has drawn.

2) The second test fit confirms progress.

4) In a power hammer, you can turn your panel upside down, or you can switch the top die for the bottom one and hammer right-side up. Andrews hammers upside-down.

5) The depression he formed, just inboard of the 90° cut, is just visible in this shot.

He continues to hammer the depression (a reverse) upside down.

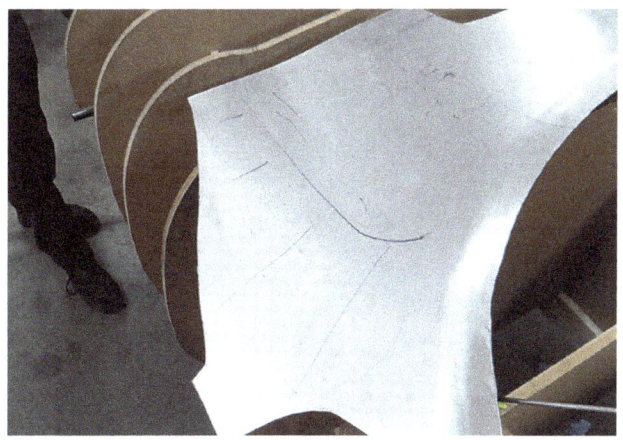
The hash marks indicate where a roll downwards must be created.

Both reverses have been shaped now.

Andrew stretches the panel adjacent to the roll. Failure to do this would cause the side of the panel to suck in when it is rolled. Extra metal is needed and stretching creates that excess.

Another test fit confirms the location of the reverses.

The roll over the side is done simply on the e-wheel with the rubber upper wheel. Done!

Chapter Seven - Part Six
AAMS Students
Lower Nose

This panel is relatively easy to form because it is a low crown. To make things interesting, Mark decided to shape the front edge using a rubber upper die over a low crown bottom die. Chris then took over and completed the panel by shaping it on the MH-37HD power hammer..

The lower nose starts as a gentle slope that drops off suddenly. Chris cuts the blank.

1) Mark shaped the end quickly with the rubber upper die. You can see the "walnuts" the die leaves in the panel. The shape came up very quickly.

3) See the dip in the middle of the panel? Whenever an edge is rolled over, a depression will happen behind it. The fix is to slightly crown the depressed area.

2) Chris took over and began to smooth out the walnuts and blend the front edge of the panel into the center.

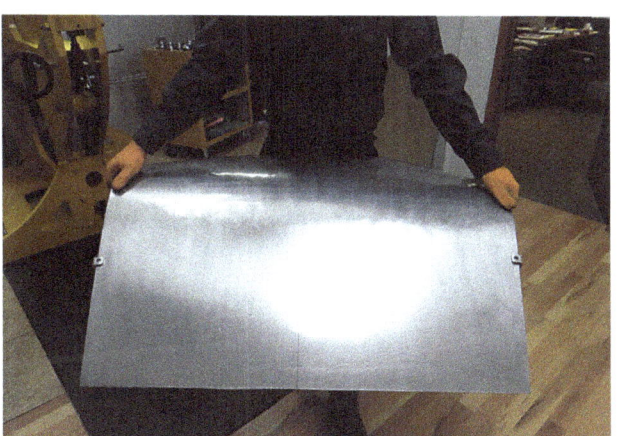

4) There is no light line here, only a light blob. That indicates a flat spot that must be raised.

5) Attending to the flat spot. Notice Chris' right hand.

He's holding on to a panel gripping clamp to keep his fingers well-away from the digit destroying dies.

Note the light lines are much improved.

The test fit is good. More planishing is needed along the lower edge.

A highly radiused lower die levels the lower edge.

Nice fit, the panel is ready to be trimmed around the snout.

Imagine going to school to learn to build cars? These Academy for the Art of Metalshaping students are!

Chapter Eight

More Cobra Panels

Mark Gerisch

In my book *Sheet Metal Fab for Car Builders* I featured Mark Gerisch creating a boot, door, and bonnet for a 427 Cobra. Because those builds were so popular amongst the many Cobra enthusiasts out there, I asked Mark to make a few more panels, this time on a power hammer. Enjoy!

Headlight to Grill Reverse - This is probably the most difficult piece to make on the whole car. Originally, a soft piece of 1100 alloy would have been slapped into a solid wooden buck to form this at AC Cars, but if you can't slap the piece into shape, you can stretch it using a power hammer or air planisher.

Danny "The Count" Koker's 427 Cobra in Las Vegas.

The most difficult shape on the Cobra, and many other cars, is the reverse between the headlight and the grill.

An accurate paper pattern is critical. Edge slits tell you where to shrink or stretch.

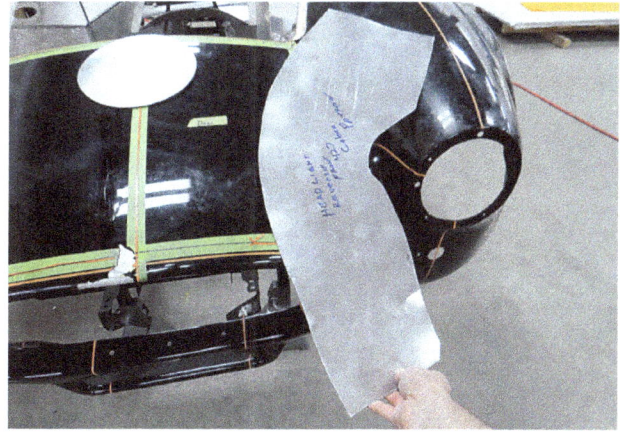

The blank must curve because you won't be able to stretch the grill side enough otherwise.

Start by using linear stretch dies along the grill edge holding the blank in the inverted position.

The panel will begin to fold, but the ends will go back. The reverse is forming.

Now stretch the headlight side, also with linear stretch dies.

More stretching on the headlight flange.

The inboard flange will mostly control the curvature of the panel.

Inverted stretching on the inboard flange.

The rubber wheel helps form the valley. In this case a high radius anvil is used.

The outer flange is preventing the panel from wrapping around. It must be stretched further…

…which is what Mark does here.

Here Mark is touching up the inner flange.

Good practice is to go back and forth between the flanges and not concentrate on just one.

The extra material at the headlight cut out is for the flange that must be turn there at the end.

Getting very close now.

So much stretching has flattened the valley somewhat. Mark redefines it.

Nit picking the details now.

He further defines it over a T-dolly.

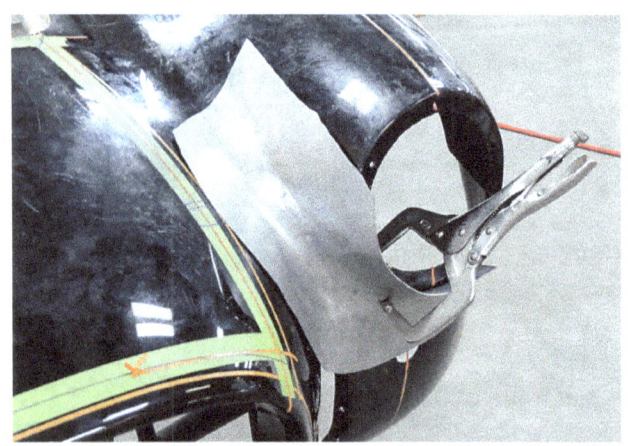

Very good fit everywhere except the bottom of the valley, which is flattish.

Light planishing removes any residual tooling marks.

Mark drives it home with some final light slapping, using a tubular slapper that he made.

Here Mark scribes a line for the headlight ring flange.

Tipping the flange along the scribed line, using the Baileigh BR-16E-36, which I consider the best bead roller available.

Mark inserts shrinking jaws into the MH-19 and power shrinks the flange to form a perfect circle.

If you look closely, you will see that Mark is using a circular aluminum pattern, where the headlight bezel ring must fit perfectly.

Chapter Eight - Part Two

The Other Headlight Panel

The next tricky panel is the one on the other side of the headlight along the front of the fender. The panel has a reverse immediately under the light that fades to flat. Here's how it's done on the power hammer.

Most of the "action" on post-war "pontoon" style cars happens between the wheel arch-headlight tube and the grill. Mark will make the piece that goes from the outside of the fender, across the headlight, and down below it to the bumper bracket opening.

The blank is prepared with accurate stretch and shrink notations, as well as the headlight location.

On the top of the fender crown he pulls some shrinks. Die changes takes seconds on the MH-37HD.

Using the rubber upper die, Mark roughs out the headlight bulge with a few blows from the power hammer.

More shrinks are made on the bottom front wheel arch.

Flipping the panel over, he switches to the linear stretch dies and expands the inside curve of the head-lamp so that it will lay flat.

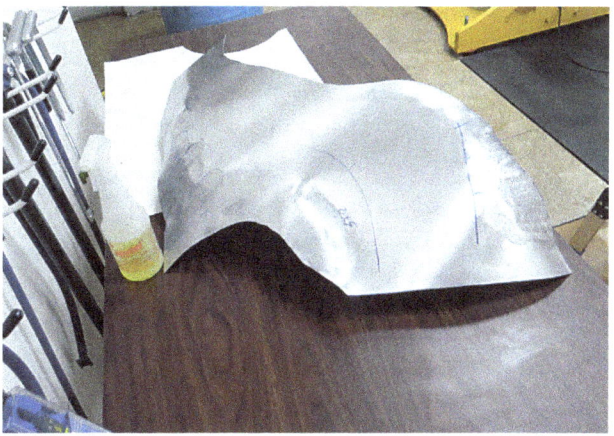
You can see all the zones Mark has worked so far. In maybe ten minutes?

101

Switching to a radius die Mark blends the shrinks into the panel.

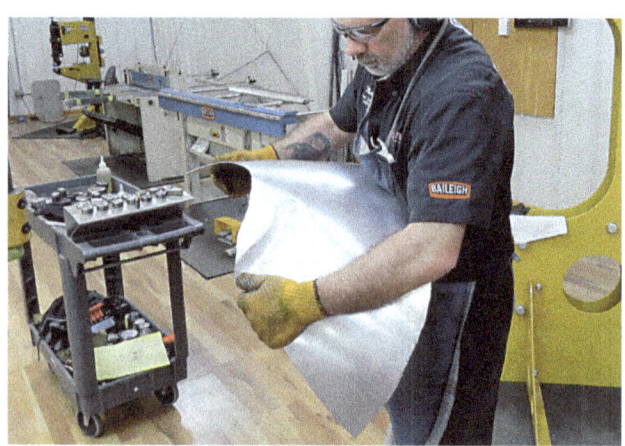

Mark forms the panel into a tighter curve.

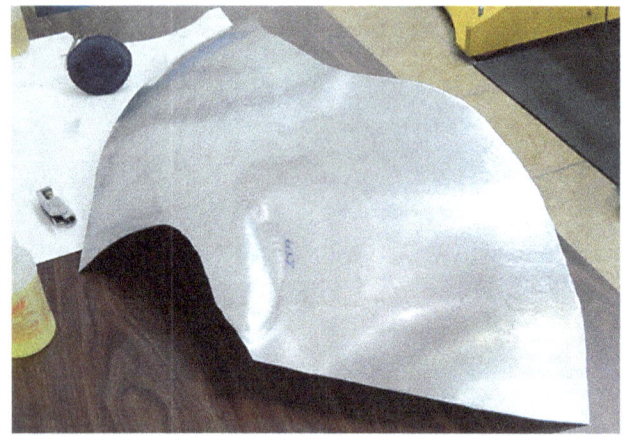

Blending leaves the panel very smooth even at this stage.

In only twenty minutes Mark is at this stage.

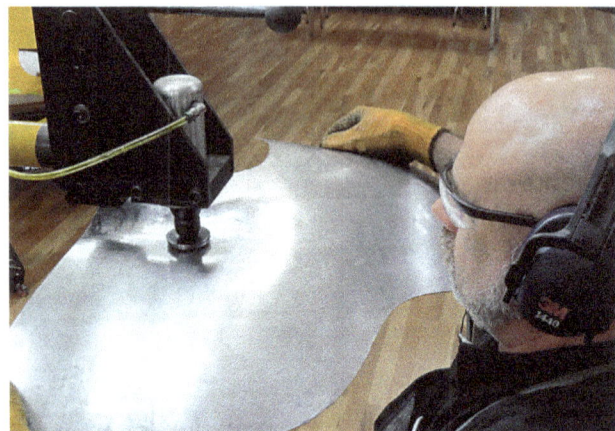

Some aggressive work on the planishing hammer helps define the flat area under the headlight.

Baileigh offers a large, medium and small set of shrinking dies for the MH-37HD. Mark chooses the smaller set for tight work around the headlight flange.

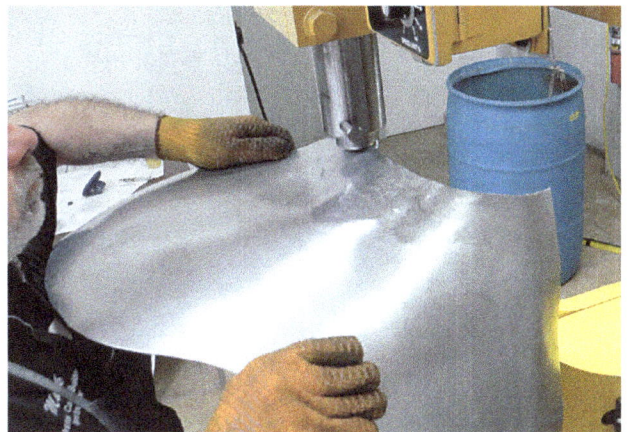

Pulling very small shrinks.

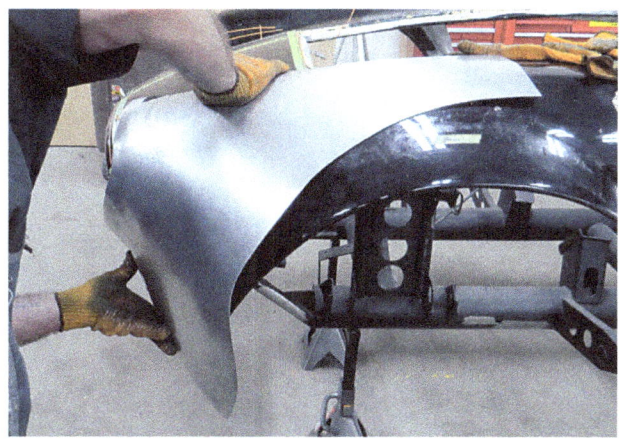

Notice how much the headlight bulge has come out. The surface finish is remarkably good, too.

The rubber wheel is a great way to precisely place addtional form into a panel.

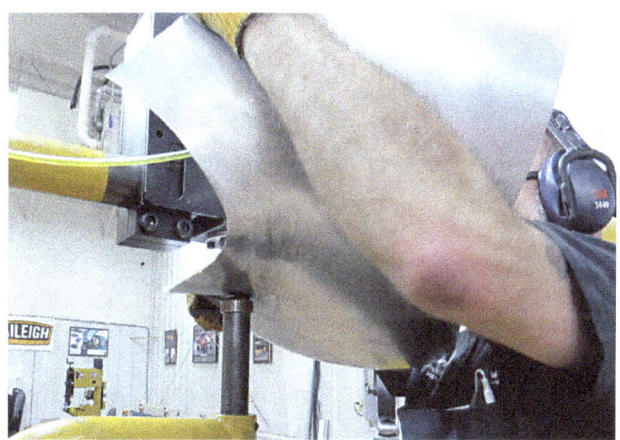

The air planisher extension on the MH-19 allows Mark to move the bulge line slightly, yet leaves a very good finish.

Inverting the panel he uses linear stretch dies to expand and move the headlight bulge.

Planishing the entire panel as it nears completion.

Test fit shows a nice fit everywhere except immediately under the headlight cutout.

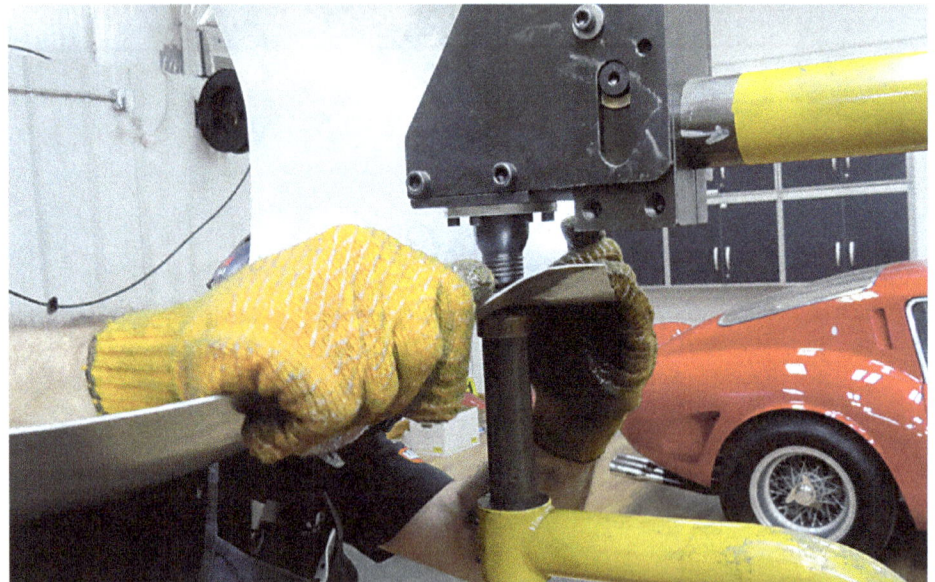

He moves the line closer with the planisher...

...now it's closer, but still out.

By now the panel has work hardened, and so Mark anneals it.

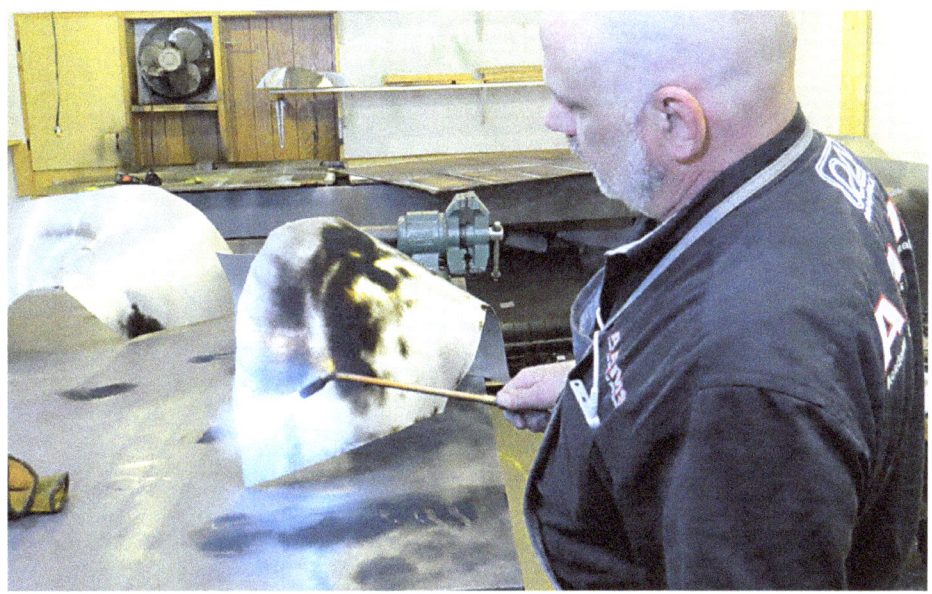

After it cools, Mark goes back to the planisher for some final detail work.

The finished panel. Total time was just under ninety minutes.

Chapter Eight - Part Three

A Metal Medley . . .
. . . in G (for Gerisch) Sharp!

Due to space limitations I cannot show you the complete sequences for each panel Mark made for the Cobra, but the following shows the key steps for the major ones. Mark is actually able, by using a power hammer, to rough out a complete Cobra body in only three days! As you work to improve your skills, don't worry about speed. Let speed come only after quality is achieved. Mark has developed his skills over the course of a four decade career so that he can produce high quality panels at high speed.

Hip Panel

The hip panel is a common to many 1950s sports cars and often involves a large reverse between the hip and the door jamb. Mark creates this hip mostly through stretching.

He lays out the pattern over the car body and notes areas where additional material must be left for turning flanging, in this case, the fender flare flange.

Using a rubber upper die and a highly crowned lower, he roughs out the shape quickly on the MH-19. The "bag of walnuts" towards the front shows where most of the crown is located.

Using the optional planisher conveniently located on the side of the MH-19, Mark makes quick work of smoothing walnuts.

The basic shape is already there in only twenty minutes of work. More stretching will be needed to "settle" the panel down onto the body buck.

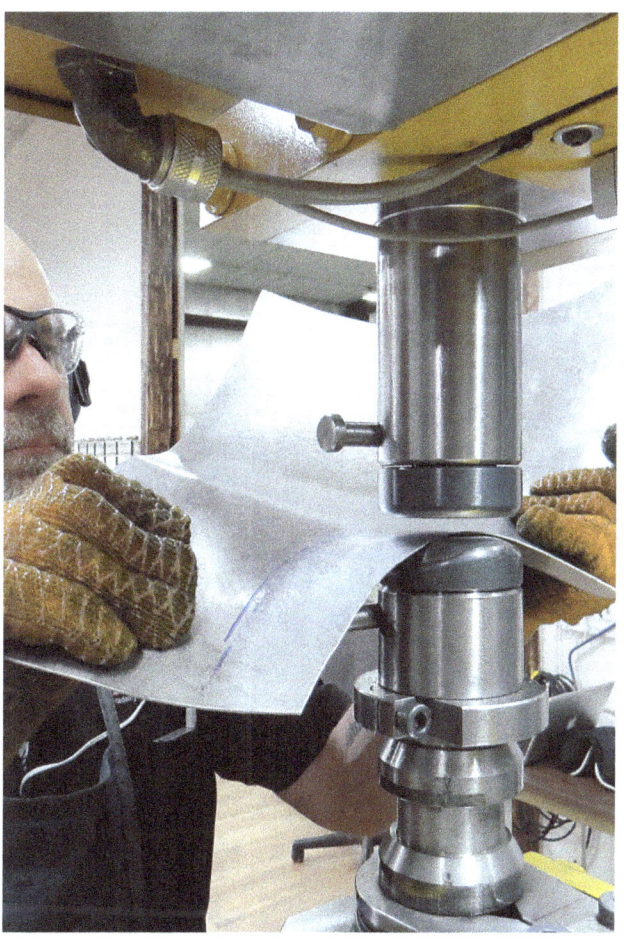

To turn the edges over into the cowl areas, he uses a liner stretch die in the MH-37. Linear dies spread out metal side-to-side. The extra area created allows the flange to be rolled over into the cockpit.

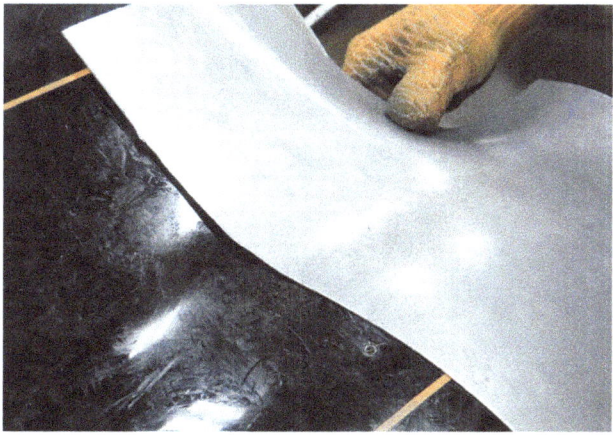

The valley in the center of the photo was created by stretching the panel upside down using the linear stretch dies.

Just over 40 minutes of work were needed to form this nicely planished, close fitting panel. On to the next one.

QUARTER PANEL This panel is a simple panel to form. It is the classic "shrink the edges, raise the center" panel, although the center is raised just a little. Final forming is done on an E-wheel using a rubber upper wheel.

This large quarter panel fits behind the hip panel and is fairly simple to make. Mark will make the passenger side panel.

Mark very lightly works into the panel to give it just enough crown. Note the special panel clips he's using to keep the two sheets together as he works.

To demonstrate the massive power of the MH-37HD, Mark decided to shape 2 panels at the same time! This was commonly done in aircraft plants during WWII to speed production. The MH-37HD is equal to any Yoder or Pettingell in brute power.

Once again, he doesn't have a half hour in the panel thus far. The majority of the curvature in the panel has been put in by folding it using a rubber upper wheel in his Baileigh EW-37.

After shrinking the edges with thumbnail dies, he blends the shrink into the center of the panel with a slightly crowned lower die and flat upper. Note the light. Good light which will show any remaining waviness in the panel.

On the buck in less than 45 minutes. The employees in AC's factory back in the '50s and '60s were paid by the piece - speed was critical. Mark is working faster than they could because he has a power hammer. The fender flare is a separate panel.

FENDER TO HOOD PANEL The best way to form this panel is to split the fender crown at its apex, then come right down to the hood opening. This requires a reverse adjacent to a high crown with a valley in between. Follow along...

This panel is one of the most intricate on the car. It has two distinct zones, the fender crown, and the hood reverse. They are separated by a valley.

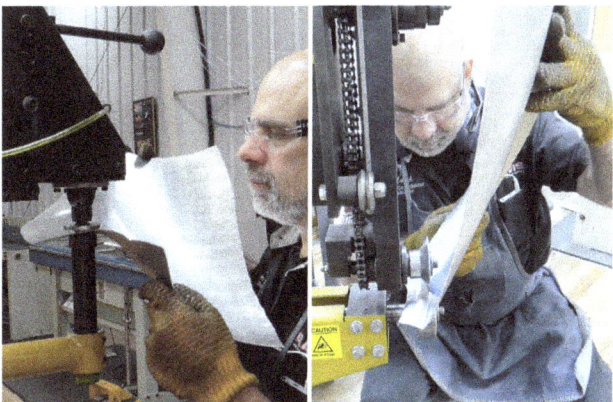

L: Final planishing is done inverted. R: Headlight ring position is scribed with the panel on the car, then tipped in using a Baileigh BR-16E-36 beading machine.

Mark laid out his panel using a paper pattern and began by shrinking the edge along the fender crown. Once again, he doing two panels at the same time.

The final positioning of the valley is accomplished by using a round bar. The valley is not a constant "V", but one that flares out towards the grille. Mark easily conforms it to the buck with this tool.

Now working on the hood edge, he uses a linear stretch dies to create more area. Note how he is slightly canting the panel upwards so that the hammer forms (sets arrangement) as it shapes (creates area).

This panel took over an hour due to its complexity and variety of shapes. The front of almost all classic cars is where you will spend the vast majority of your time.

It's the intent of the author and publisher of this book to celebrate and advance the art of metal shaping - as practiced and demonstrated by the following artists, each of whom gave freely of their time and expertise.

Baileigh Industrial Tools
www.baileighindustrial.com

Dave Byron, Spence Industries
Spenceindustries98@gmail.com

Tommy Caruso,
Contour Metalshaping
www.contourmetalshaping.com

Jack Charles,
Lakeside Technical College
william.charles@gotoltc.edu

Jamie Downie, Kustom Garage
www.kustomgarage.com.au

Stan Fulton Fulton Metal Works
sfulton@casscomm.com

Jeb Greenstone,
Cutworm Customs
www.cutwormspecialties.com

Kyle Yocum
Yocum's Signature Hot Rods
www.Yocumsrodshop.com

Mark Gerisch, Academy for the
Art of Metal Shaping
www.aametalshaping.com

Ron Covell
www.covell.biz

Ron Fournier
www.FournierEnterprises.com

Craig Naff
Woodstock, Virginia

Mark Naglich, Lakeside Rod
and Custom
360-871-1185

Austin Paruch, Paruch
Automotive Craftsmanship
Austin-Lee@hotmail.com

Mike Phillips, Phillips Hot Rod
& Customs
www.phillipsautomotiverepair.com

Chris Rusch RMD
www.rmdbenders.com

Wray Schelin
www.proshaper.com

Mike Wagner, Cornfield Customs
Cornfield_customs@hotmail.com

Kent White
www.tinmantech.com

111

Chapter Nine

A Flare for Metal

Mike Phillips

Mike Phillips is typical of the new generation of metalshapers in that as a kid he was inspired by the car and motorcycle reality TV shows where outsized, smack-talking characters build a fabulous machine in an hour and sell it for a small fortune before the last commercial break. Unlike many of his generation, however, Mike knew that "reality TV" isn't real, and that if he wanted to become a successful metal craftsman first he'd have to establish a business to support him as he learned the skills to live his dream.

Dreams can come true if you work hard enough,

This highly customized Datsun Z has been widened by Mike and requires all new fender flares.

and Mike, along with his wife and business partner Stacy, worked long and hard to establish an auto repair business which he was eventually able to expand into a performance and customizing shop, Phillips Hot Rod & Customs of Downingtown, Pennsylvania. Mike's passion is metal work, and so while his auto repair techs kept busy with customer cars Mike showed me the process of making custom fender flares. These require an infinite amount of attention to detail as they continually change shape and direction.

Stacy and Mike Phillips, partners who planned for success.

Mike's Top Tips

1. Work all areas of a panel gradually. Don't stay in just one area.
2. Problems caused by too much stretching with a radial die are easy to fix. Problems caused by too much linear stretching are hard to fix.
3. Linear dies fool you because they seem to do nothing for a while, and then all of a sudden the shape appears. Go slowly!
4. Keep linear dies perpendicular in curves.
5. Do as little planishing as possible.
6. Trust in your panel layout marks.
7. Always allow ¾" (20mm) extra to allow for smearing edge of panel in hammer.
8. When a panel being held properly jumps between the dies, it means it's time to change the lower die to a different radius.
9. Oil helps you visualize your tracking patterns.
10. Use a 2" (52mm) planishing die to pre-stretch beads.

A fender flare is a complex, meandering reverse curve that leaves no room for mistakes. These temporary tabs help Mike determine topography of the flare so his paper pattern is accurate.

The upper line delineates the flare-to-body "flat" area. The line below it is the "valley" of the flare. Positioning these lines takes time and will determine the success of the flare.

Mike learned from Peter Tomassini how to cut openings in the pattern so as to tape it to aluminum. Peter's work is featured in detail in my two other metal books.

The 3003-14 .050 aluminum blank ready for shaping, which will mostly be stretching.

He uses a snap punch to transfer the lines on the pattern to the aluminum blank.

Notice the witness line near Mike's left middle finger. It is important to test fit the flare to the same point each time.

Then he joins the marks using ¼" (6mm) painter's tape.

He transfers the "valley" location to the back of the blank. Notice the large collar he welded to his divider to accommodate a Sharpie.

Baileigh offers a rubber upper wheel option for its EW-37HD English wheel which Mike now installs in conjunction with a highly radiused lower anvil. Here he wipes the anvil with solvent to remove dust.

The easy part of the job is done. Now the "legs" have to be brought back to the car. This will be done by mostly stretching along the edges near the body line.

By following his tape line the valley is impressed into the panel easily and accurately.

Don't randomly stretch an edge. Pre-plan and do it evenly. Mike carefully marks his blank with his stretching plan.

This is not a "shaping" operation, but a "forming" one. No new "area" is created, only the "arrangement" of the panel is affected. In essence, the panel is being folded.

This is a linear stretch die. For clarity for the reader, Mike marked in black the area that actually contacts the blank. The blue along the sides are not used at all. The area between the black and blue allows for the blank to curve down.

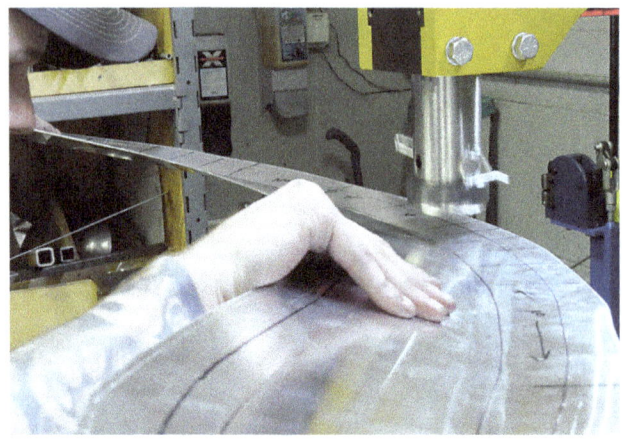

Linear stretch dies are usually used in conjunction with a flat upper die as seen here. Mike urges operators to always keep linear dies perpendicular to a curve.

Stretching along the sharpest curves on the lower edge of the panel. The MH-19 is set to moderate power during stretching operations on aluminum.

On long, floppy panels it is necessary to pull down slightly on the ends to prevent "dancing" between the dies. Notice Mike's hand position.

The die marks clearly show that Mike is following his plan. Shaping is a constant play between hammering, and test fittings. This flare required about three dozen test fits to get right.

This is the front edge of the flare where it bends towards the lower spoiler. By stretching slightly here the end of the panel curves downwards, and up.

Look carefully and notice the waviness of the edge of the panel. This means more "area" has been created there. That area will fan out thus forming the curve.

You should never shape just one area of a panel at a time. Best practice is to constantly work around the panel and bring the entire shape up gradually. Here Mike works the lower center.

A check on the paper pattern confirms valley and flange positions. It's easy to forget or get slightly misaligned at this point.

This might look close, but it's only about half way there. A finished flare should be held in place with only light pressure of one finger on each hand. Anything more and it requires more work - true of any panel.

Stretching along the flange line. Notice closely spaced hands to prevent dancing. Mike's dialed down the speed of the MH-19 for more gentle hits here.

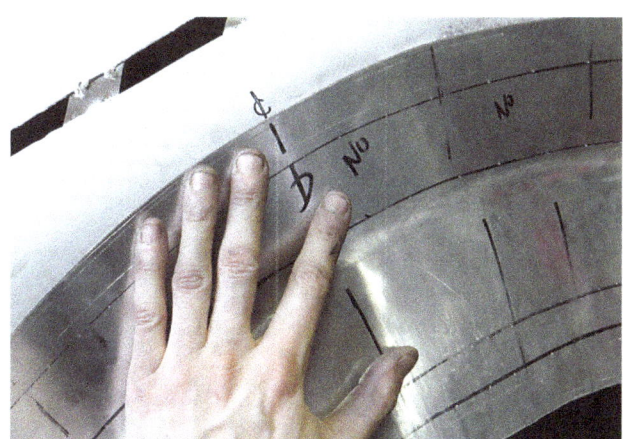

To the right of the witness line are reminders to Mike not to stretch those sectors. Mike calls them "No fly zones."

Since the actual car is the buck, Mike can only check clearances by getting up under the flare and looking for light to shine through any gaps.

Shrinking dies of hardened tool steel come standard with the MH-19 hammer.

Then he uses the sharp edge of a machine table to slightly push a crease into the aluminum.

Changing them out takes only seconds using simple hitch pins.

He feels he lost some of the valley during the shrinking operation so he renews it on the English wheel, using the rubber upper wheel.

Mike pulls a shrink at the end of the line he drew to locate the body line.

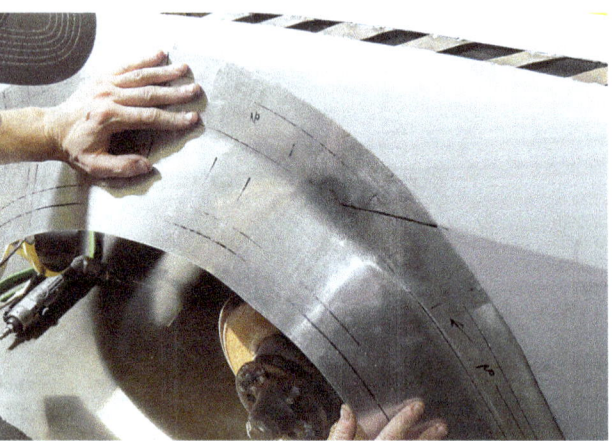

The test fit confirms the flare has now settled over the body line top and bottom.

118

Spot shrinking deeply into the panel helps to absorb a slight bubble.

It is time to blend the areas of the flare, which he will do with these stretching dies. The circle shows the actual contact area.

The flare above the body line fits well enough to be Clecoed in place while Mike marks an area to be stretched to force the lower leg towards the body.

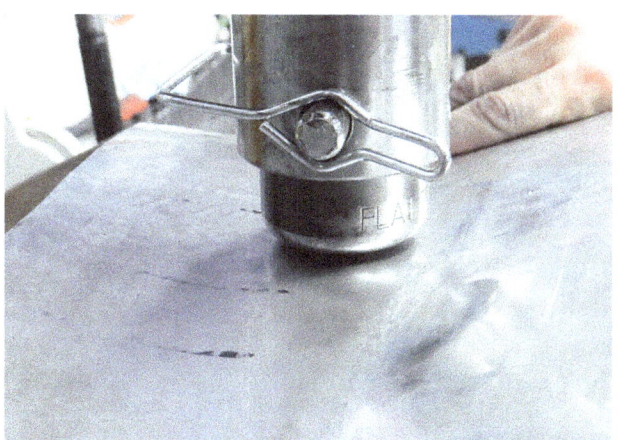

Blending should be done as methodically as any other power hammer operation. Do not just randomly pass your work between the dies, do it with lowered speed and over-lapping blows.

Before removing the panel he uses a length of pipe to better define the valley.

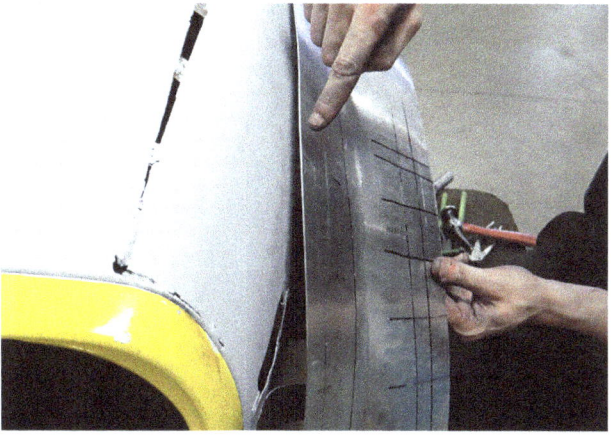

Mike points to a "tight" area which needs more shaping to bring out.

He stretches that area with the linear stretch dies. Notice how he curls his panel to prevent a ridge line forming. Refer to Tommy Caruso's chapter.

The fit is 99% there, which means it's time for planishing.

Another test fit.

Rapid strokes, but with dies close together, is the best method to produce a good finish. Open die jaws tend to shape, rather than planish. Lower die is 6" (150mm) radius, top is flat.

Fine-tuning the valley once again.

Scribing the flange line.

Tipping the line on a bead roller. Make several passes, not just one.

A light sanding with a DA removes any tooling marks.

The panel fits exactly and can be either riveted on, or welded.

Chapter Ten

Saving Edison's Car

Kyle Yocum

What can you say about a young man who is only in his mid-20s yet received a commission to build panels for a piece of national treasure? You'd have to say he's not only good, he's one of the best. Kyle Yocum is that young man and right out of high school his one and only goal was to open his own hot rod and custom car shop. Along the way he worked at a restoration shop which was the focus of a reality TV show, but quickly tiring of the staged drama Kyle left to open *Yocum's Signature Hot Rods* in Suffolk, Virginia. He hasn't looked back.

Charles Edison was the son of Thomas Edison

1936 Brewster Ford Town Car. Luxury on a budget during the Great Depression. Photo courtesy Gabor Mayer / Hyman Ltd. Classic Cars

light bulb, phonograph, etc. - and himself earned a reputation as an astute businessman, philanthropist, and incorruptible politician. Though wealthy, he was prudent and during the Great Depression owned a chauffeur driven 1936 Brewster-Ford Town Car. These cars were budget limousines in that they featured coachbuilt Brewster bodies over ordinary Ford V-8 drive trains.

Edison died in 1969 but his car survived, and is headed towards the Edison National Historic Site in West Orange New Jersey. B.R.Howard & Associates, who are conserving the car, approached Kyle to create new fenders to replace the original rusted ones. The fenders themselves are a gushing last hurrah of "art nouveau" styling in a world that was rapidly turning to streamlining. The magnificent "fluttering ribbon" under the fender's edging is also seen on the Mercedes-Benz 540K. (See p. 105 of my book *Sheet Metal Fab for Car Builders*).

The mounting flanges of the fenders were merely lag-bolted to the wooden frame of the Brewster body. As they flexed, water became trapped and ate the flange over time.

Even Edison's father couldn't invent something better than a paper pattern to plan a panel.

*Kyle Yocum, center, and the crew at **Yocum Signature Hot Rods**, Walt Maddox (l) and Joshua "JP" Phillips (r). Yeah, you've seen them on TV.*

The bottom of the panel, with its many magnets, indicates where most of the stretching needs to happen. The fender is a very graceful reverse curve, so both edges will have to be stretched.

The yellow tape indicates highlight lines.

He checks the blank against the buck to assure it is large enough.

Kett shears easily trim the panel. Kyle likes a 1" (26mm) (extra) border around the blank.

The first operation is to stretch the inboard edge. Good light is critical and Kyle surrounds his MH-19 with shop lights.

It took Kyle four days to build this buck and fair it. Typical, a buck will be fairer than the original panel.

Linear stretch dies will rapidly expand an edge and raise a reverse. Push-pins are no longer used on new MH-19s, and older models, like Kyle's, can be upgraded from the factory for free.

With just a few passes Kyle has the reverse just starting to appear. Not the slight dip in the center.

A test fit on the buck confirms things are heading the right way. From original photos of the car it looks like there is very little shape in this pane. In fact, there are no flat sections.

Notice the two lines of hash-marks close to Kyle. He will stretch the inboard curve to create the subtle reverse, but later come back and aggressively shrink the outer edge to drop it down. Slowly working all areas of the panel again and again is the key to success.

More linear stretching.

Curling the panel and pulling down helps prevent the panel from "dancing" and also prevents a ridgeline from forming when he releases it.

The inner edge reverse is obvious. The outer edge is flying high and will need shrinking.

Die changes take seconds on the MH-19…

Kyle recommends repeated oiling of the panel top and bottom during shaping. He believes a side benefit to oiling is that it acts as a hydraulic cushion which decreases tool marking.

…as does adjusting tool height…

Using a wider set of linear stretch dies he blends into the panel. When blending a shrunken edge, work towards the center of the panel.

…using a crank wheel and locking arm.

As the edge is raised, the rest of the panels begins to settle on the buck.

Fay Butler markets a line of profile gauges that help determine the best die set to use. Always use the least aggressive.

The linear stretch die is oriented 90° to precisely follow the line. On traditional power hammers this would necessitate either a separate die, or the time consuming task of repositioning the tool holder.

Top and bottom dies are interchangeable on the MH-19 and can also be oriented 90° from normal. Thus reverses can be formed without the need to invert the panel.

Another test fit shows the panel is close, and it's time to shrink the top.

When an edge of a panel becomes slightly wavy, hammer just inboard of it to tighten it. It is best practice to avoid hammering edges unless forming reverses.

Shrink dies are installed.

*Notice Kyle's grip on the forward edge of the panel. Both hands are pulling down slightly as he shrinks. This force helps **form** the panel as the hammer **shapes** it.*

The final shape is beginning to appear.

Your intrepid author has a go at shrinking.

Blending begins using the 36" radius die.

Kyle has shrunk at least a foot (300mm) into the panel. Tooling marks are minimal.

Within minutes the shrinking marks are mostly gone. Kyle's attention to panel lubrication pays off.

"Art nouveau" was the application of floral forms to man-made objects. The Brewster fenders were meant to evoke a tulip or lily petal.

Blending the shrink ridge back into the panel with radius dies.

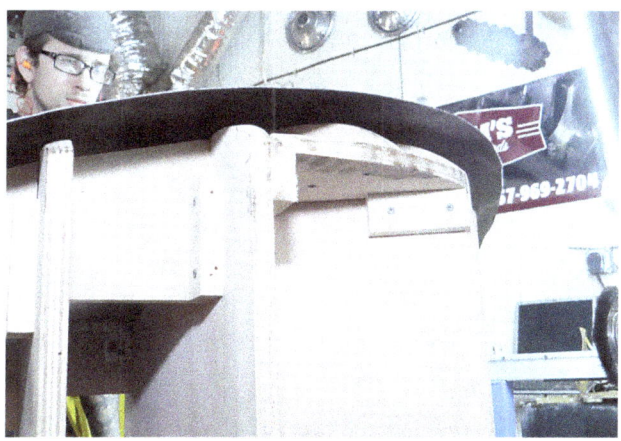

The test fit shows a fender that is not down on the buck yet...

Kyle points to a "tight" area that is hitting the buck. He'll hammer this to create more area so the panel will settle to the buck.

...but it's nothing that a little more shrinking can't handle.

After hammering, the panel fits with a loosely set clamp. The upper edge is still too high as seen by the gap on the right.

Kyle shrinks and blends once again.

Barely visible on the left are two screws holding the panel in position as Kyle checks it. At this point in its creation, a panel should always maintain a position or else you'll never settle it 100%.

It's an advantage to have the original part still in gloss paint, to check during the work. Highlight lines on the new panel should be the same as on the original. Yellow tape marks separate panels for the new fender.

The inner corner is still about 5/8" (15mm) off the buck. Kyle feels the planishing process will bring it down.

Nit-picking the outer edge. Notice lift of inner right corner. He'll stretch this to bring it down.

Kyle planishes the entire panel with his vintage Chicago Pneumatic machine.

Planishing serves to stress-relieve a panel as well as smooth out any imperfections. Tooling marks are of little concern on a panel that will be painted.

The valley is another subtle reverse. The outer edge requires shrinking to bring it over.

The next panel is the one that dives towards the running board. Notice the two lines of shrinking he has completed. The panel was inverted while shrinking the inboard edge.

When a panel requires very subtle transitions, the hammer should be set on its closest stroke. The motor speed is controlled by a dial selector on the front of the machine, as well as a foot control. Variable speed is a huge benefit available on modern power hammers.

Kyle blends the various zones with radiused dies.

More stretching is required to bring this area down prior to welding and flanging.

With a raised center section as seen here, Kyle decides not to shrink the edge over, but to stretch just inboard.

The front triangular panel was formed through crowning on the hammer and planishing.

Stretching the inner corner with an aggressive linear die. Note inverted panel.

Moving on to the fender's edge "ribbon" Kyle now converts his MH-19 to a reciprocating machine by inserting a pin in its upper connecting rod. Using Delrin® dies he cut himself he profiles the ribbon. INSET: Close up of the profiling tool.

Rear panel is ready to be planished.

Next, he flanges it. INSET: Close-up of the flanging tool. The tipped line is very crisp and will receive the wire for a wired edge.

Kyle uses traditional hand tools to initially trap the wire.

The ribbon is temporarily Clecoed in place. A cut line is then scribed and it is finish welded in place.

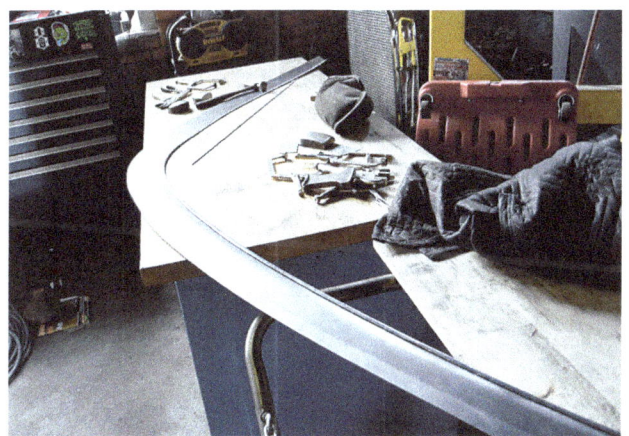
Wire edging is laborious, but necessary. The tool Dave Byron developed is therefore worth considering. See chapter 13 for details.

Brian Howard, project coordinator, supervises Kyle's team with the installation on the car.

Closing the edge of the flange tightly over the wire with Pullmax-style dies. This leaves a very neat installation.

Yet to be painted, the Brewster Ford looks like its slicing through water. Who says they don't build 'em like they used to?

Chapter Eleven

"Art Rods"

Jeb Greenstone

The mountains of western North Carolina are the home to a growing artistic scene. Centered in Asheville, millennial painters, musicians, and sculptors gather in this beautiful, green region inspired by its natural beauty, and solitary remoteness. What Jeb Greenstone creates in his shop in the even more remote town of Hayesville has gained a reputation for its aesthetic quality. Jeb doesn't build rat rods, or traditional hot rods, or custom cars - he builds something just a bit beyond. The cars Jeb turns out from his shop *Cutworm Specialties* have become known amongst his admirers as "art rods". They are "Carolina cool".

This very unusual truck is another unique Cutworm creation.

Jeb's coachbuilding skills are mostly self-taught. The only lessons he's had were when friends dropped by and offered tips. Not a trained artist, or designer, Jeb's vision is guided by one credo: "If I've seen it before I won't do it." Because of that *Cutworm* rods are always unique. In the following sequence Jeb makes a highly shaped fender for a one-of-a-kind rear engined Hayabusa powered hot rod-track car.

By the way, "Cutworm" was the nick-name given to his grandfather by his football teammates back in the '30s. No one knows why!

The Hayabusa powerplant mated to a Quaife differential is expected to push the car to over 130mph (200kmph).

"Art rodder" Jeb Greenstone.

Jeb created a very sculpted fender mock-up from cardboard. Intended to be a track car, brake cooling is critical so a big duct was cut out.

Every panel begins with paper. Just inboard of the wheel arch is a massive reverse. Openings in paper show stretch areas. This panel is not easy!

The MH-19 is extremely easy to adjust. You can increase or decrease power by simply cranking the lower wheel and locking down the upper handle.

Jeb stomp-shears the blank of 3003-H14 .063 aluminum.

Jeb's practice is to set the die gap by pulling a piece of material through them. When the piece just begins to drag, the gap is good.

Although more time consuming, Jeb prefers to file a panel edge rather than use a deburring tool. Different strokes for different blokes.

The built-in indicator shows the stroke to be .4 inches (10mm).

This removable wheel adjusts the stroke.

He manipulates the panel back to roughly flat to assess the shrink.

Oil is squirted on both sides of the panel.

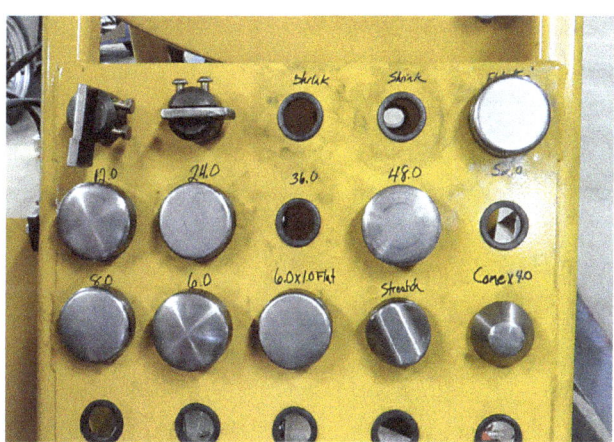
Baileigh offers a large range of tooling, although anyone with a lathe can easily turn custom dies. Note the upper left pair. These are used when the machine is locked in reciprocating mode.

The thumbnail shrinking dies follow a carefully marked plan on the panel. Jeb does not "free-style" shrink. Notice his hands are curling the panel, and pulling down slightly.

Jeb switches over to a linear stretch die to begin the reverse. Die changes take a few seconds with no further adjustment necessary.

By stretching the edge while the panel is inverted, a reverse appears very quickly. Alternatively he could have switched the lower die with the upper and worked the panel right-side up.

By stretching this area it was driven down. Jeb's finger is above the transition point between the shrunk and stretched areas. Only good planning can get this type of accuracy.

There are three control inputs on the MH-19. Stroke, tool height, and hammer speed. None of them require tools to adjust. When you find the "sweet spot", very little tool marking is visible.

Now Jeb begins to work the reverse on the other side of the panel.

When working a reverse your hands need to impart a force to form the metal as you shape it. Here Jeb sweeps the panel through the dies.

It didn't take long for this panel to take shape. The front and back are heading the right way, while the outer edge needs more shrink.

The best practice is to bring up all shape transitions gradually, so Jeb blends areas together first with his radius dies.

He points to the area that requires more raising.

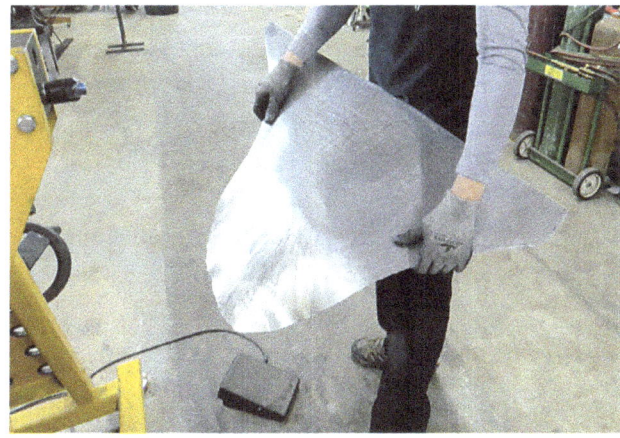

The foot pedal controls hammer speed through an electronic box connected to the Variable Frequency Drive (VFD) DC motor. Hammer speed affects hammer force.

Another test fit shows there is still a gap under the front edge as well as the outer edge. The best way to lower those is to raise the center.

More blending and smoothing. Jeb works the panel upside-down here. A flat die is on the lower tool holder and a radius up top.

Using reduced power he carefully raises the center of the panel.

*Jeb is building this twin-turboed Ford Coyote 5.0 rod for a customer. Check out the wheels which were created entirely in-house at **Cutworm**!*

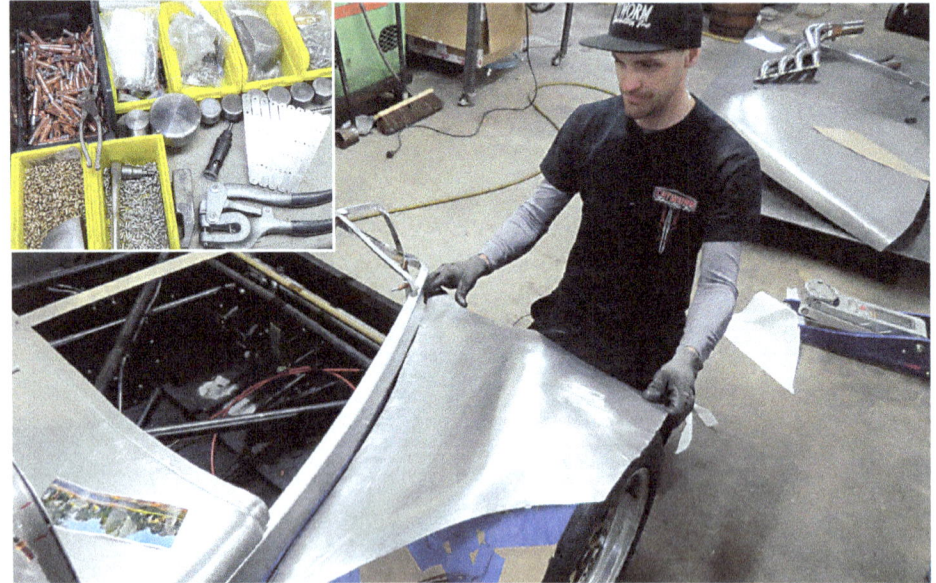

After trimming the inner edge of the panel to follow the contour of the body, the fit is good. However, in raising the center of the wheel arch the peak has kicked out rather than heading straight back. INSET: Jeb often uses aircraft tools and fasteners to put his cars together. It creates a lighter, yet stronger, joint…not to mention one that is more artistically pleasing.

Jeb quickly remedies the peak by redirecting in with a teardrop mallet in a sandbag.

Jeb planishes the reformed area in the air planisher he designed and built using a Michigan Pneumatic power head.

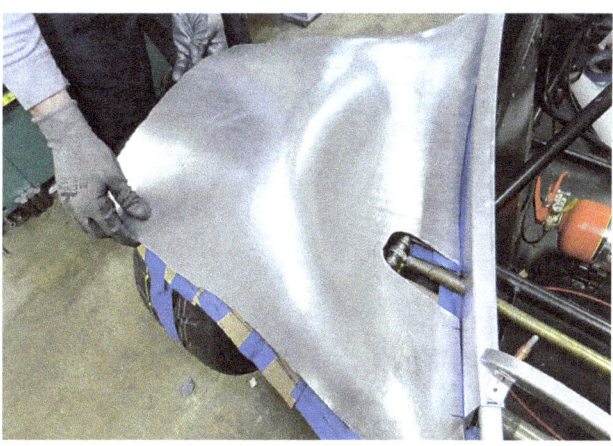

Now the panel falls into place easily.

The panel has all the required shape, but needs a complete planish and final trim. The rear is sitting high because of interference with the upper suspension.

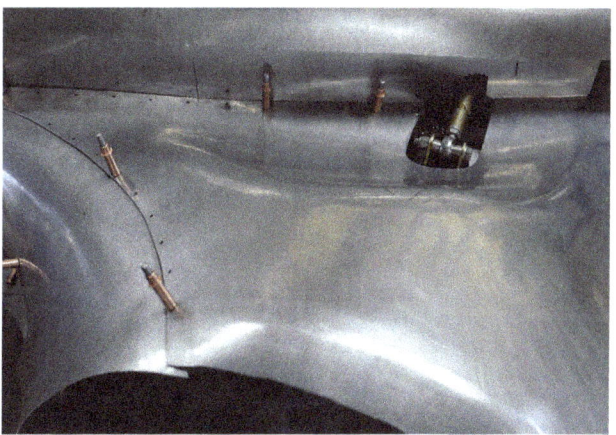

Nearing completion, the panel's outer edge is shrunk over prior to wiring, and the inner edge stretched up. The rear panel has also been made and is mostly the result of stretching edges. The upper and lower "legs" of it are really reverses inside out.

An air nibbler is used to create a cut-out.

*Another **Cutworm** "art rod" comes together.*

Chapter Twelve

Power Driven

Dave Byron

Dave Byron started working with metal as a hobby, but he worked so diligently to teach himself all aspects of it from machining to sheet metal work that it became a business. *Spence Industries, Inc.* in Green Bay specializes in custom hot rod and motorcycle projects. Four years ago Dave took the plunge and purchased a MH-19 hammer. His skills as a panel beater improved rapidly so that now his work can now be seen in multi-million dollar car collections.

Dave Byron's **Spence Industries** *specializes in custom fabrication of hot rods and motorcycles, which is just fine with shop mascot Vincent.*

Badly damaged '39-53 Indian sidecar with a fore-deck in need of a replacement.

Some metalshapers prefer to call a reverse curve a "reverse curse". Why? They're hard to do because they are tricky to visualize. The metal isn't being worked one way as in a crown, it is worked two ways, two curves curling away from each other. The most important thing to remember in any shaping project is: With a crown you stretch the middle, with a reverse you stretch the edges. This is true whether you're forming with a mallet on a stake, in an English wheel, or with a power hammer.

Here's how Dave recreated a '39-53 Indian sidecar.

A paper patter was made over the buck, and its lines transferred to a blank of 19 gauge steel which Dave trims to shape on a B-2 Beverly shear.

Simple buck of MDF. Your panels will be no more accurate than the buck they are made on.

Dave's practice is to crush panel edges on his English wheel before using a deburring tool.

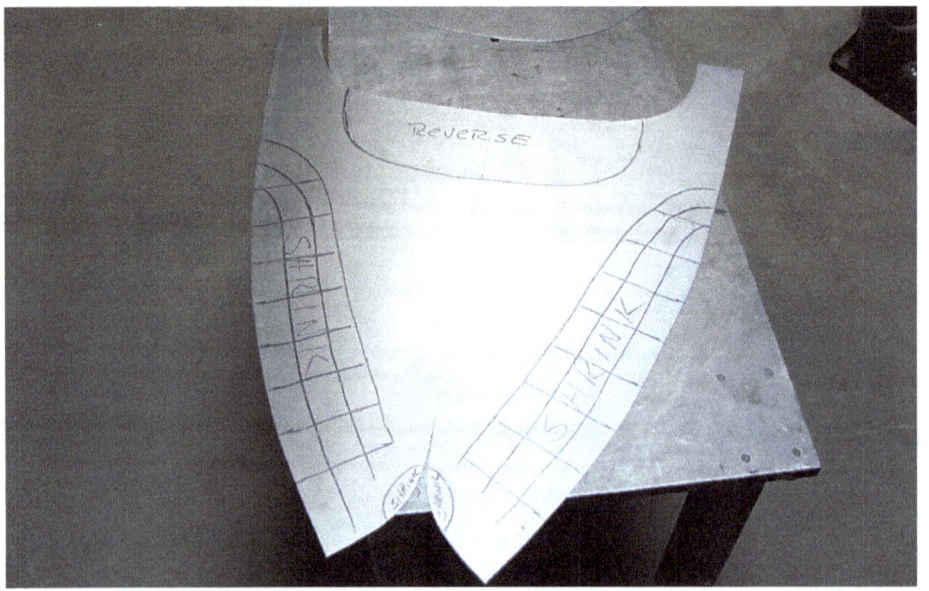

Power hammer work requires a plan, and here is Dave's. The three rows of boxes represent how far into the panel Dave will make each shrink, starting with the deepest rows.

The brake creates the center crease in the foredeck. This crease was in lieu of a strengthening rib.

Panels tend to curl into a ball when shrunk. They must be opened after each operation.

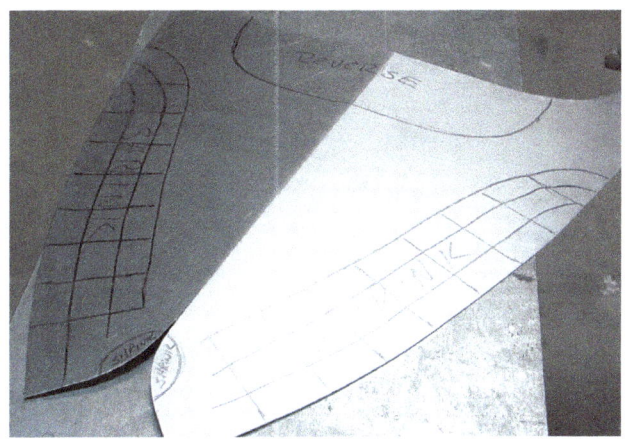

The panel ready to be shaped.

Going in the right direction. Notice how the shrink "fades out" toward the cockpit opening.

A large, and small set of thumbnail shrinking dies are available for the MH-19.

A slight shrink is needed at the bottom of the "v" in the nose. Note the machine's fence drawn back to the frame. It can be set for precision reciprocating work.

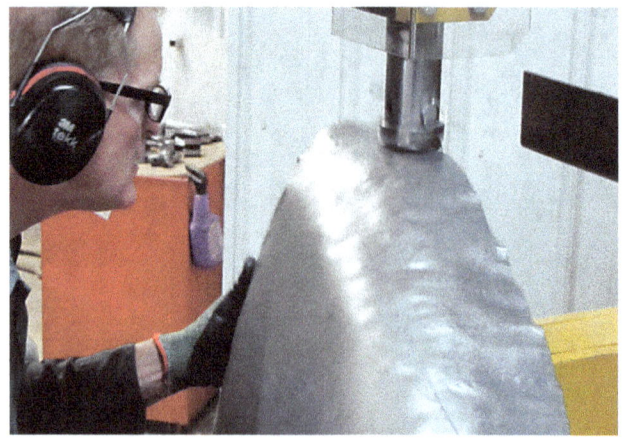

The final row of shrinks is made along the edge.

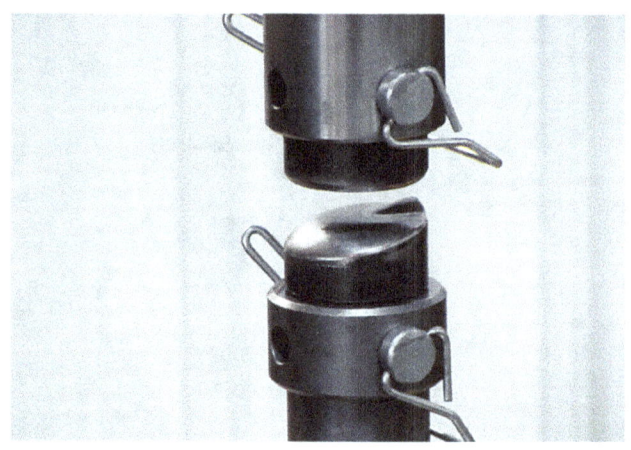

Dave inserts the small thumbnail shrinking dies now for fine tuning of the panel.

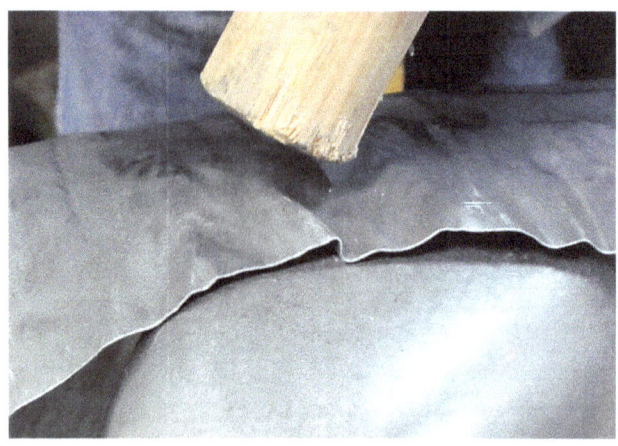

Any time a shrink is in danger of folding over on its self, it should be realigned as Dave does here using a wooden mallet on a cast iron forming head.

He evens the bottom edge through careful, medium powered shrinking. Shrinking is easy on this machine because of the VFD (variable frequency drive) DC motor.

As shown, the replacement nose is much more settled on the buck.

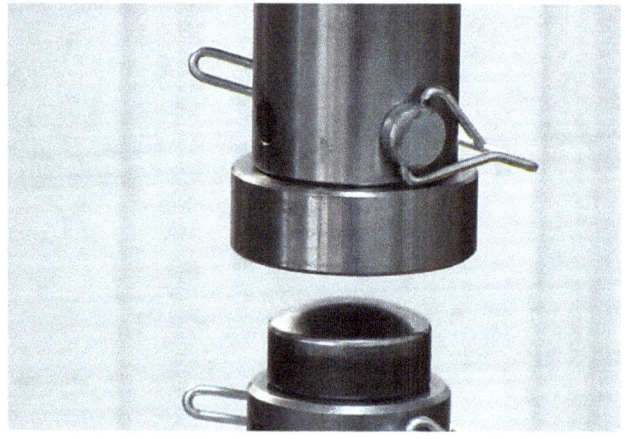

He changes to small planishing dies. Match the radius of the die as closely as possible to the radius of the panel.

Using slow speed and closely spaced dies, he begins planishing.

Planishing has helped, but the body will require some stretching over the shrink lines.

Dave had originally intended to try to create the wind deflector directly on the foredeck panel, but found that a separate panel was required. Here is the blank cut out.

Reverses are either stretched on the edge, or shrunk in the middle, or, a little of both.

Dave begins by persuading each edge downward over forming head.

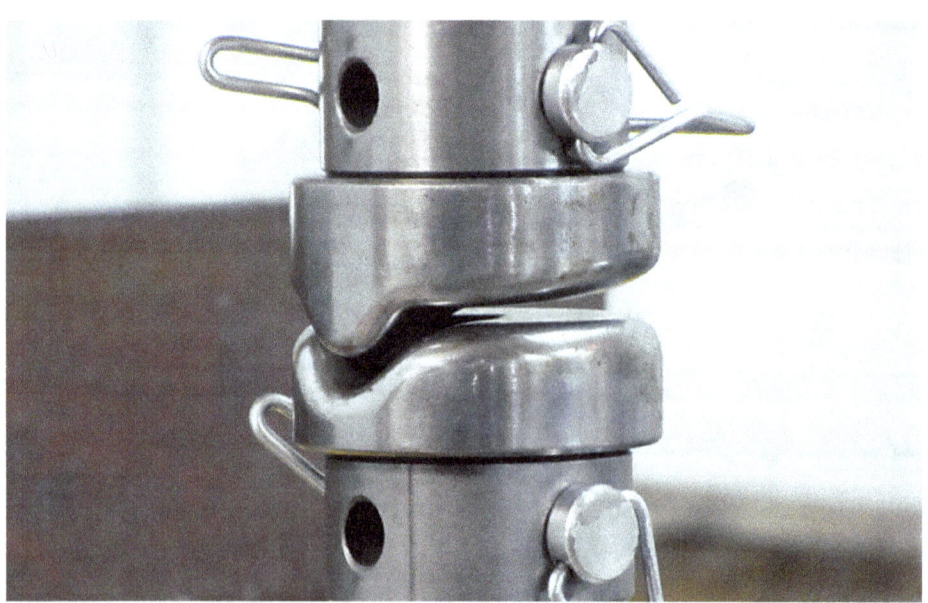

One of his interesting metal shaping discoveries is that shrinking dies can be used right through the middle of a panel from axis to axis. He prefers to invert his dies for this.

The panel is curled as the shrink is made down the center.

And uses them to begin stretching the edges.

After three passes the reverse is taking shape.

More edge stretching is done over a forming head.

Very mild linear stretching dies are now installed.

"Chinese wheeling" (inverted) serves to planish the panel.

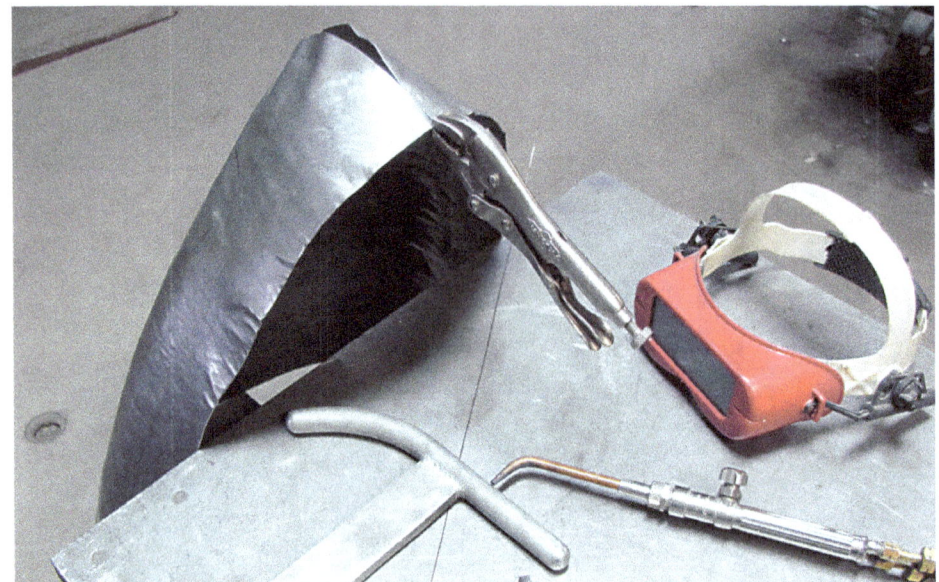

The nose of the foredeck is prepared for welding.

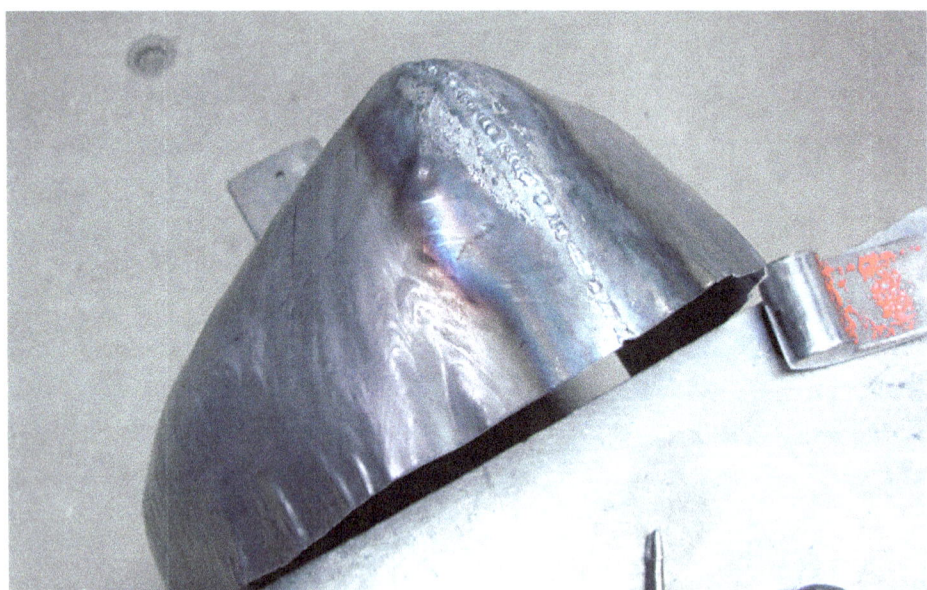

Notice that the end of the weld has not burned away and is as solid as the rest of the seam.

A test fit over the deteriorated original foredeck shows a very close fit. INSET: Dave used this Ron Fournier T-dolly to planish the welded nose of the foredeck.

By shrinking the center of the panel rather than relying solely on stretching the edges, Dave has maintained the panel's edge thickness, and therefore its strength.

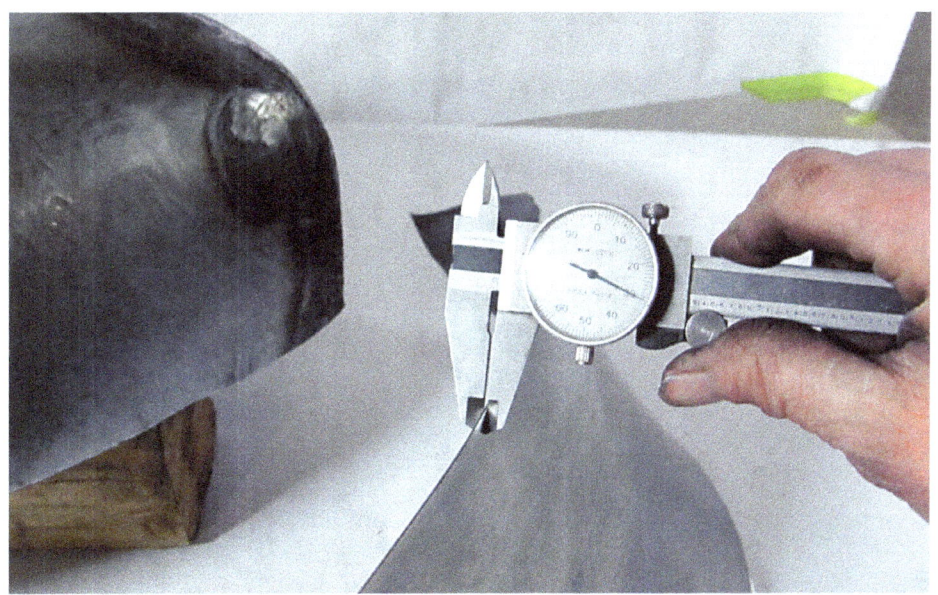

The two pieces ready to be welded together.

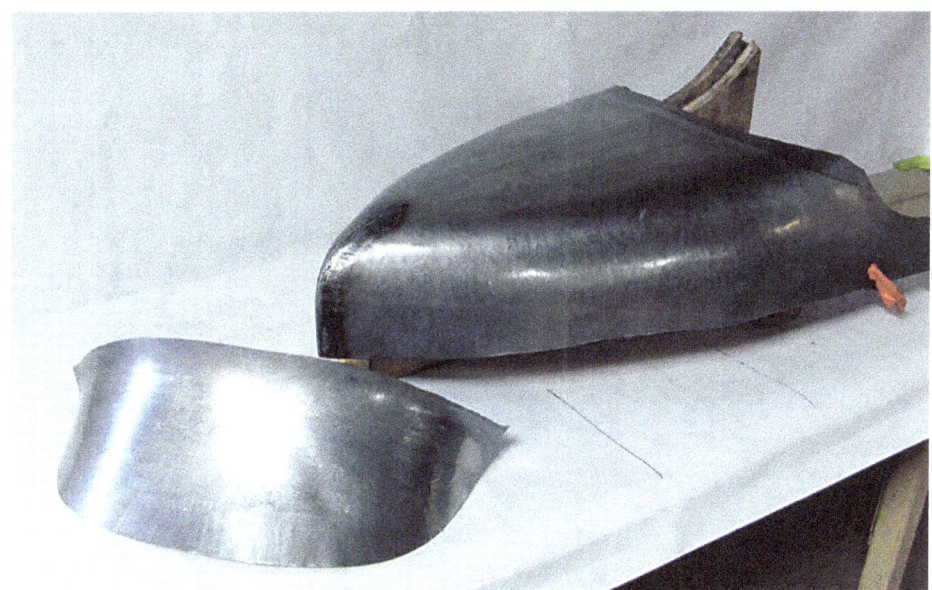

After welding he expands the weld line using a very small stroke and low speed.

Dave uses tape to locate the final cut line on the deck and the wire edge flange along the deflector.

(Left) What every metalshaper needs! Dave developed this die set which folds over, and closes a wire edge very quickly, relieving much of the drudgery of this necessary task.
(Right) The upper die is relocated along the holder four times during this process and locked in place with a bolt (not seen in this photo.) This is the second position.

(Left) Third position.
(Right) Fourth position.

The final position of Dave's dies traps the wire tightly.

Dave has the MH-19 set to reciprocating mode while using his wiring dies. He prefers the MH-19 to his Pullmax because the stroke and the speed can be set very low for fine work.

The old and the new foredecks.

Chapter Thirteen

Home-made Diamond Plate

Tips from Don Houseman

You have seen the Pullmax reciprocating machine in use in several of the shops featured in this book. A Pullmax, a mini-Pullmax, or an MH-19 power hammer set in recip. mode are must-haves for any serious panel builder.

Don Houseman once owned a metal fabrication business in Watsonville, California and knows all about the many, many ways to shape metal. His hobby is custom and race car fabrication (Bonneville Racing). After being diagnosed with multiple

Master fabricator Don Houseman and his retro-look hot rod.

sclerosis in 2002 he does this work as a hobby and to keep challenging his body and brain.

We featured a few of Don's techniques in Sheet Metal Fab for Car Builders, but Don's metal fab knowledge is so deep that we could devote an entire book exploring his Pullmax methods. Here are two more clever ideas from a master of that machine. The first one shows how Don made a new running board for an ultra-are Graham pickup truck. The Graham brothers supplied trucks to Dodge who marketed them in the 1920s.

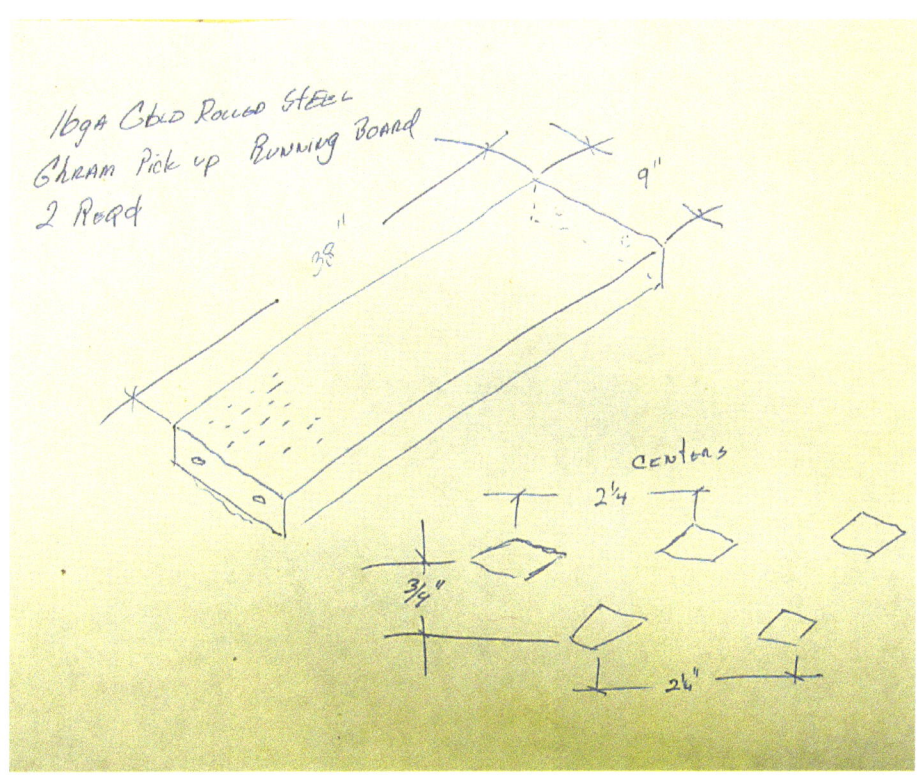

The customer supplied dimension of the running board. Replicating the diamond tread pattern is the hard part.

Don's rigged his Pullmax with an air foot pedal that lowers the top tool holder. The pedal allows him to keep two hands on the work.

Don cut these die to stamp the pattern, with a variety of milling tools, grinders, and hand files. Profiling the diamond correctly required many test punches.

1) Careful marking is critical to an evenly spaced pattern. One false move and you start again.

3) The finished running board. The Dodge and Graham brothers would be very pleased!

2) Every other line is pressed longitudinally and laterally.

Perfect Pullmax Dies
with Kirksite

Getting an exact Pullmax die profile is difficult and time consuming when using a metal cutting band saw, grinders, and hand files. Don shows us the easy, fast, and 100% perfect fit method using Kirksite, a compound of mostly zinc that melts at a low temperature, and solidifies quickly.

In this sequence Don reproduces the belt molding for a '34 Ford roadster pickup. He shows us how he made dies that reproduced the bead perfectly.

Kirksite is a zinc alloy that melts at only 800°F (425°C) but solidifies quickly into a substance as hard as steel. It cost only about $7.00 per pound, is easily cast into complex shapes, and can be reused infinitely.

1) To start, a wire contour gauge finds the profile of the old running board.

2) It is used to make a paper pattern which is checked against the running board. ¾" (20mm) addition is left above the bead to serve as a reservoir so the Pullmax mounting plates have something to bolt into.

3) After transferring the pattern to an 18 gauge blank, it is trimmed to size with a B2 Beverly shear.

4) Internal areas are trimmed out with a rotary punch before being hand filed to an exact fit.

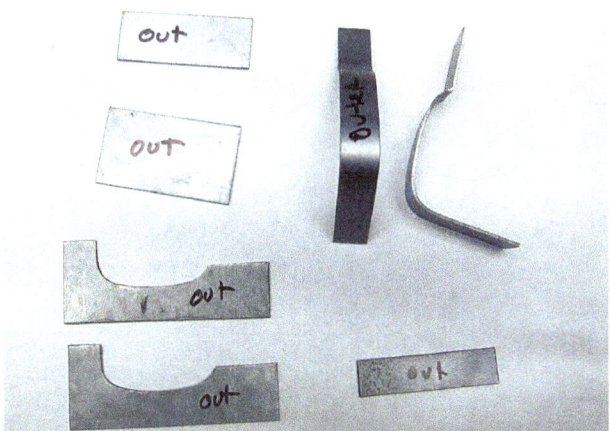

These are all the pieces needed for the topside (outer) die.

And the topside (outer) die in place.

They are TIG welded together. Only a few tacks are necessary.

Four clamps are needed to keep it tight to the bead so as to prevent leakage.

Here you see the underside (inner) die in place.

A blast of carburizing soot is shot into the form to serve as a release agent.

The Kirksite is melted in a plumber's pot using a rosebud torch tip to melt it quickly. Skim the slag off as it melts.

It takes about 20 minutes to cool, and when it does you have two perfect molds properly spaced thanks to the thickness of the original steel. Note a little seepage on the left die. It shaves off with a knife.

The heavily sooted mold.

The two dies must now be milled so as to have a parallel top and bottom.

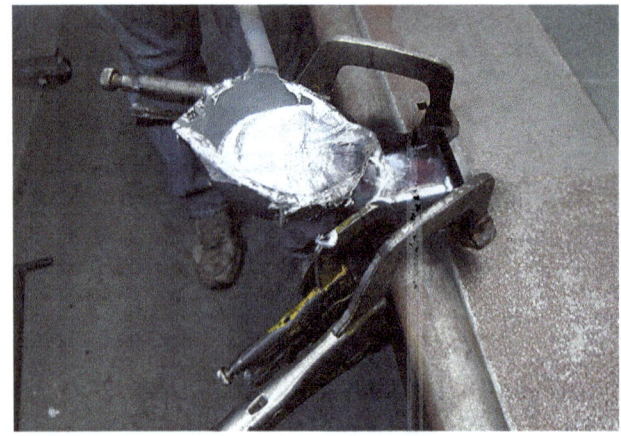

Kirksite is then ladled into each form.

Don mills the molds, and then pre-drills them for the Pullmax mounts.

Here they are, bolted into the Pullmax mounts.

The Pullmax is dialed in loosely for the first few passes.

Rounding the edges with a belt sander. The feed-in edge is more highly rounded than the exit.

Then it is cranked down for the final pass.

A test blank is pre-bent on a brake.

A final test fit with the contour gauge confirms the shape. Note the excellent finish. Some operators oil the blank before passing it through the dies, but Kirksite is slick enough that oil isn't necessary.

Chapter Fourteen

Welding What You Hammer

Gas and TIG Welding Tips

The oxy-acetylene welding torch was invented in France in 1900 and it was quickly adopted on both sides of the Atlantic. It was exactly at this time that coach building also transitioned from wood to metal and the industry needed a way to stick panels together. Electric welding had actually appeared a generation before gas, but the early machines were not very controllable, The electrical supply varied dramatically from city to city, and fluxed rods, though available, were primitive affairs coated with crude compounds like clay slurry. Gas welding, though difficult to learn, was able to produce reliable welds whether or not the shop had access to electricity. It became widespread after the invention of the welding tank in the U.S. in 1913.

There are two types of regulators, single and dual stage. If you have problems with steady flow, get the dual stage, like these Craftsman.

Therefore, during the entire age of fine coach building, from 1919 through the 1960s, all the great bespoke bodies were welded together using gas. All of them. Even when the first primitive MIG welders appeared in the 1920s, and the technicians at Northrup Aircraft in California invented Heliarc (TIG) welding in 1942, gas welding remained the process of choice for panel beaters.

Shapers will debate what is the best way today to weld panels together, especially aluminum panels. You can separate the top-notch wheelmen who have contributed to this book into two vociferous camps Gas vs. TIG. I'm going to put my foot down, however, and say that purely from a technical stand point, gas welding is the better way to join panels. Why? Because of something called the heat affected zone. On either side of a welded joint you can actually see the HAZ because of the panel discoloration, particularly in steel panels. TIG and MIG have much narrower HAZs than gas welds. Because a weld always affects the molecular structure of a panel, and tends to harden it right at the join line, a gas weld is the preferred method because the wider HAZ acts as a long damper on the stressed weld line. Think of it as a rubber motor mount versus a solid one. Gas welds are less likely to crack than TIG welds. Gas welded seams are much easier to crush or planish with a hammer and dolly because they're softer. More importantly the U.S. based Aluminum Association Inc. which works to promote a wider adoption of aluminum products around the world, has exhaustively tested electrically welded joints and concluded that they suffer from a lack of density compared to gas welded joints. This explains why TIG-welded tanks are far more prone to leaks than gas welded ones. Kent White, who not only is a brilliant panel beater, but also holds the rare distinction of being a certified Boeing instructor, alerted me to these tests and further stated that even today major aircraft manufacturers are leery of TIGed joints.

Now, notice how earlier I said "from a technical stand point". In the real world, gas welding is messier than using TIG because of the use of flux and the need to wash it off immediately after welding. A bit of flux grit can ruin hammer dies and your e- wheel's anvils during the weld crushing process. TIG welding often seems easier to set up, especially when you're

All my gas connections use these quick-connects from Radnor. Swapping torches and hoses is a snap.

A gas saver is a good investment with the increasing price of gasses.

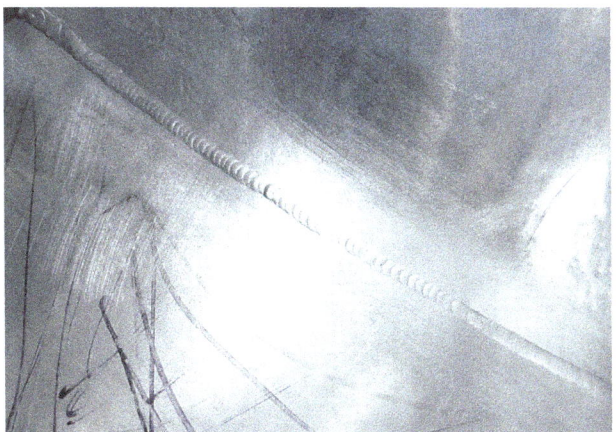

Kent White laid down this bead. It is consistent, fully penetrated, and not too high. This is your goal.

The weight of the torch is less important than the weight of the hose dragging it down. Kent White's Ultra Light Weight hose is well worth the small cost.

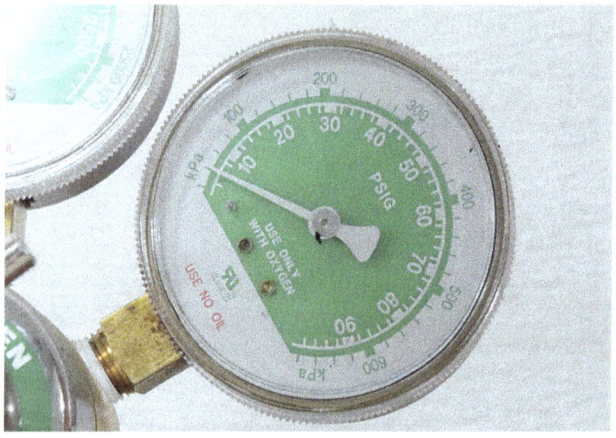

If you're using a Dillon-type, you can set your regulators down to 4 psi each. The Meco Midget is 2psi! Others torches are typically 6 psi. I've even seen, depending on the welder, 25 psi used!

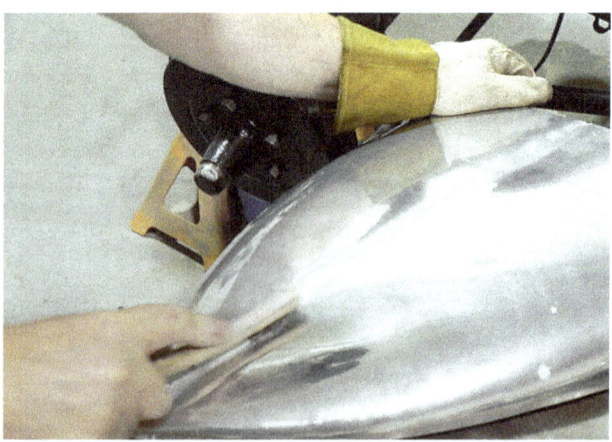

Ron Fournier, another gas welding master, uses a stainless steel brush to clean the oxides off the weld line on both sides. Oxides cause sluggish or lousy puddle flow.

just running a series of tack welds. However, the REAL reason many fabricators opt for TIG over gas is that they don't practice enough with gas to stay good at welding with it. That is the bottom line. In the coachbuilding era welders were, by union rules, an entirely separate trade from panel beaters and therefore welded day in and day out. Men who welded panels didn't hammer them. They were full time pros who maintained their proficiency. It's hard for a person running a one-man business, or a weekend DIYer, to develop and retain the requisite skills for gas welding. Northrup developed TIG in the heat of WWII so that less skilled factory workers like Rosie the Riveter's sister, Wendy the Welder, could keep the production line moving. Gas welding has always been the most difficult of the processes to learn.

Having said that, let me say that a good panel man who is conscientious about his work can use TIG to build a car that isn't going to vibrate apart as it goes down the road. Good welding practice gives you a fully penetrated panel whether you're using gas or TIG. Cleanliness of the weld and penetration are actually more important factors than Gas or TIG. WELD more, Worry less!

Oxy-Acetylene Welding

Gas steel welding is easy to learn because of the obvious color change of the weld puddle, so I'm going to only describe aluminum which isn't easy. Many newbie aluminum welders think the trick to welding this temperamental material is to go at it very slowly with a small torch and low heat. This approach usually doesn't work because aluminum wicks heat away from the join line very, very quickly. After waiting a long time for the puddle to get hot enough, the welder lays down his first bead, but then finds the panel is too hot and collapses all of a sudden. The reason is that during all that waiting time the rest of the panel has been loading up with heat and is ready to drop as the welder lingers over that first tack.

A better technique is to go in with a hotter, larger flame and bring the weld puddle up to heat quickly before the rest of the panel heats up. Once you get the first bead down, you scoot along shoving in filler rod. Typically, you have to move faster and faster the longer you're on a panel. The only way to learn this is to practice again and again.

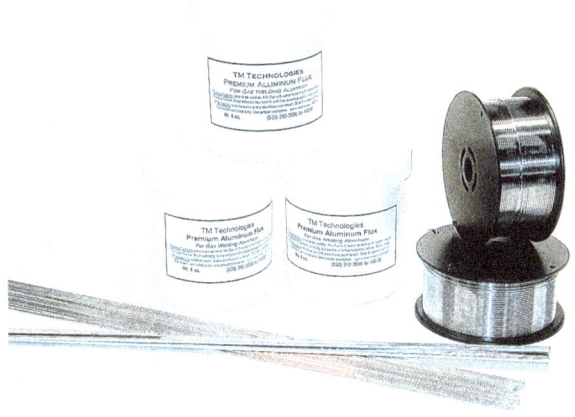

Flux is getting hard to find, try Kent White. Mix it with bottled spring water to a thin paste. If welding aluminum be sure you use the correct flux because some other types have too high a melting point while brazing fluxes contain zinc chloride which ruins gas welds.

Kent White's TM 2000 lenses are the best you can get to combat flux's orange glare. Traditional cobalt lens are cheaper and available in the U.S. from Ron Fournier.

Murex is an excellent flux available in Europe. An acid brush with a stainless handle is the ideal applicator.

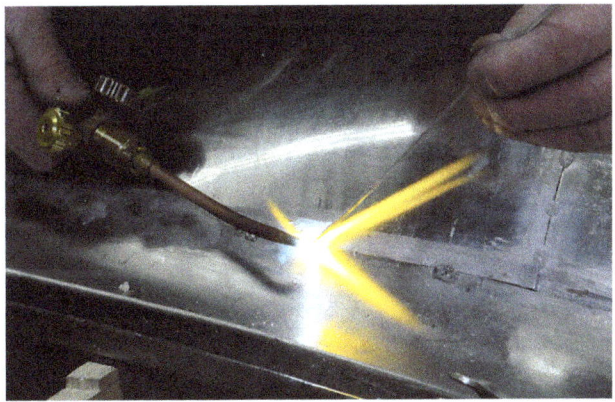

Welding steel panels is easy because of the noticeable color change. Aluminum welding is much harder because there is no color change, only a momentary texture change of the weld pool. Note the typical orange flux glare.

Heat your panels, and your filler rod just a bit, and brush on the flux paste as Mark Barton is doing here. Don't inhale the fumes.

Most would-be aluminum welders fail because they don't set the torch well. Pros like Mark go in hot and fast.

Start by tacking ¾" (18mm) in from the ends and then tack every ½ inch.

On aluminum, once you've let your panel cool, splash some vinegar on the weld seam to neutralize the flux and then hose and brush it using plenty of fresh water.

You must adjust the panel gap to zero before each tack. Mark uses a scribe to pry up a panel. Dental picks also work well.

Use a hammer and dolly, or slapper (flipper) and dolly, on the weld join to lift and level the shrinkage due to welding.

A tight fitting strip of thin copper under the ends of the panel makes welding them much easier. The real trick to aluminum welding is learning to heat 'n lift, heat 'n lift… especially to control heat at the ends.

Mark still uses this flipper he made as an apprentice. Note the perfect balance, which means it won't tire his hand if he uses it for extended periods.

A faster method for re-stretching shrunken welds is to wheel them in a machine as Ron does here in his Quick Shaper. An air planisher also works. INSET: This custom anvil at The Panel Shop is used only to stretch welds and can get into tight corners.

The traditional finish for a welded aluminum panel seam is to brush it with a stiff, stainless steel brush. Use only stainless. 26. INSET: Snap-On Tools sells this stainless brush set.

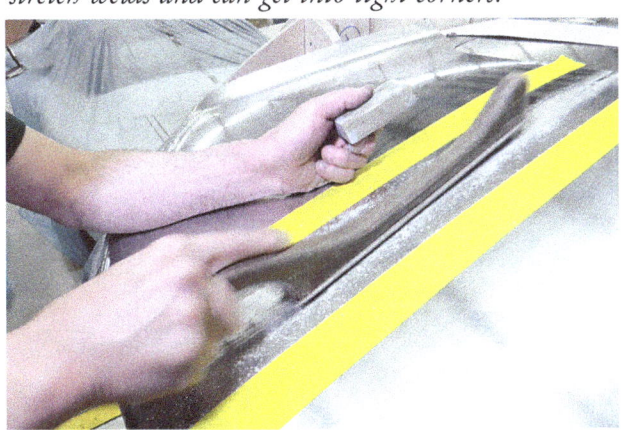

Use a body file to flatten lumps in the filler. Soap (in Mark's left hand) lubricates the panel and prevents chips clogging the file.

The results are very pleasing.

Once the seam is nearly flat, any extra filler should be sanded off using 50 or 80 grit discs. INSET: Wray Schelin recommends cutting corners into a sanding disc so it will be more flexible and less prone to gall a panel.

How do you get good? Do like Kent White and practice, practice, practice.

TIG Welding

TIG welding is very frustrating for newbies too, especially because there are so many conflicting methods of doing it and every welder you talk to knows that his way is the way to do it. Some of those methods are decidedly outdated. Again, steel is much easier so I'm only going to describe the aluminum process.

If you've already got an older TIG welder, you've probably been using a pure Tungsten (Green) electrode and balling the tip. Good, keep doing that. However, if you don't have a machine yet I strongly recommend you invest in one of the new inverter TIGs. They are much more portable and friendly to the use of Ceriated (Orange) and Lanthanated (Gold) electrodes. These newer types can be used on steel or aluminum, don't need balling, only sharpening, and they don't contain radioactive material. What's not to like? Well, the new electrodes cost more than tungsten types, but when you factor in their more forgiving nature, and ability to go both ways, steel and aluminum,

A good auto-darkening helmet and lots of light greatly aid TIG welding.

the cost is very justified. There's no need to ball them, just sharpen them 2 ½ times electrode width, much like a sharp pencil in miniature. A 3/32 inch size is pretty standard for panel work. I strongly recommend you spend a few dollars to outfit your torch with a gas lens. The laminar gas flow from this upgrade makes welding easier. Also, get rid of your argon regulator and use an argon flowmeter. The best TIG-man I ever witnessed, Al Waite, told me that controlling flow is much more accurate than regulating pressure and the savings in argon the first two bottles will pay for the flowmeter. He points out that gauge settings vary greatly from set-up to set-up, and recommends finding the flow setting that works most efficiently for your particular set of tank, flowmeter, torch, and lens.

Use a stainless brush to clean the front and back of the weld seam. Drag a Scotchbrite® along the filler rod, or MIG wire.

As in gas welding, you've got to start with a scrupulously clean seam. Use a stainless steel brush on both sides of the panel to clean a ½ inch (13mm) path along the edge. Drag a clean Scotchbrite pad over your filler rod. Aluminum MIG wire is often used. Set your amperage to the thickness of your panel. For instance, an .063 panel needs about 63 amps, an .040 40 amps, etc.

Use an auto-darkening welding helmet, but it real-

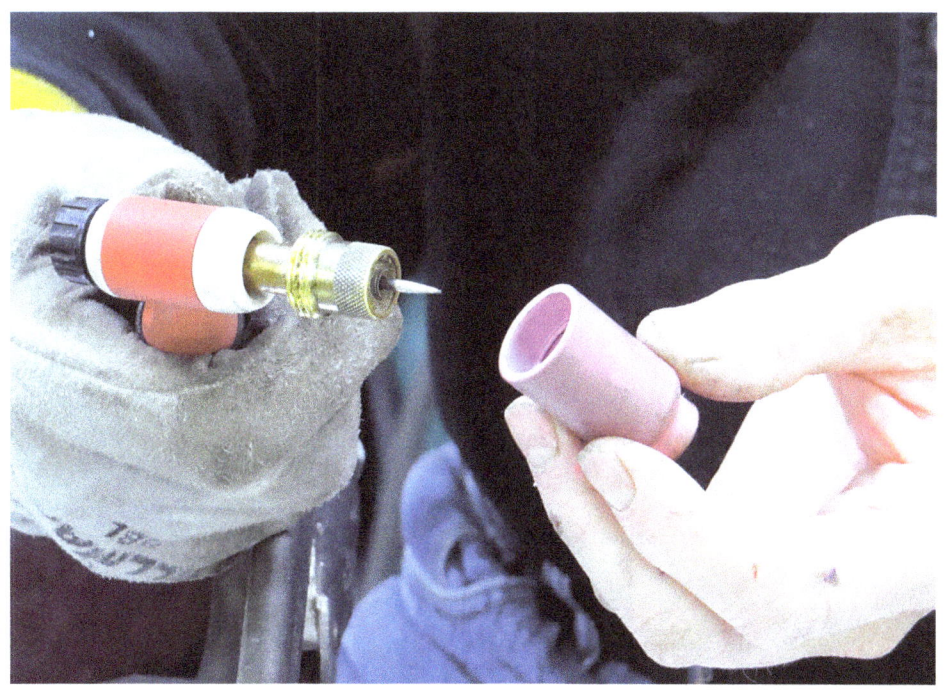

A gas lens is an inexpensive useful upgrade to your TIG torch. It eliminates the argon's turbulence and settles it to a laminar flow.

169

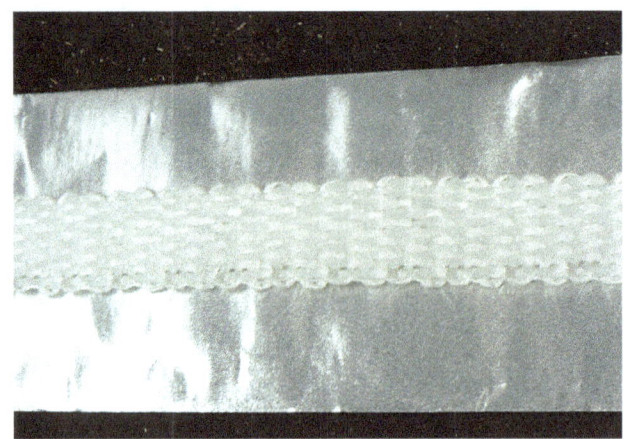

1inch (26mm) fiber glass tape can be applied to the back of a weld seam using aluminized HVAC tape.

Back up the end of a weld with a copper strip to help absorb heat and prevent a blow-through.

Even professional welders like Jordan Scowary try to rest both elbows while TIGing.

ly helps to light the panel using high power lamps, not just your shop's fluorescents. If your eyes are getting old, use diopters (reading glass lens) inside your helmet. Again, as with gas welding, one of the biggest mistakes is to try to sneak up on the panel. Go after it with heat! You don't need flux. A significantly improved weld seam will be attained if you cover its back side with either a copper strip, or with a length of header wrap taped on using aluminized insulation tape.

In some super high-tech applications welders go so far as to plumb their back cover strip with a separate argon line and feed purging gas in. This is overkill for most body panel applications, but keeping air off the back by covering it is not. Practice is the only short cut to success. Kent White strongly recommends welding both the front, and the back, of a TIGed joint to achieve full penetration.

TIG welding with your elbows in the air is extremely difficult, but not impossible as Steve Hall proves as he welds this Ferrari 275 door. He's using a thumb controller instead of a more common foot pedal.

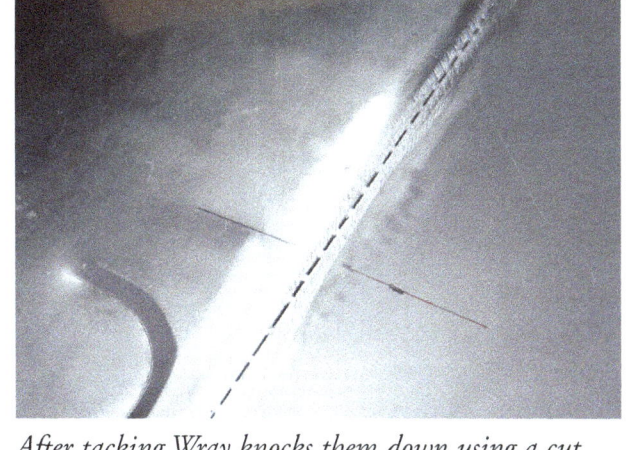

After tacking Wray knocks them down using a cut off sanding disc and winds up with a perfectly flat seam ready for final welding.

Ever gotten a TIG shock due to a poor ground connection? Guess why I'm wearing not only gloves, but welding sleeves as I zip up this Bugatti Type 52 tail.

After planishing the tack line Wray finish welds it. Here he climbs up a flange.

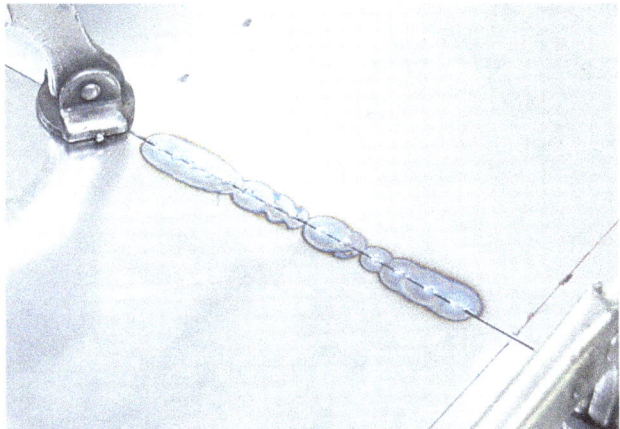

Lots of people say a ¾" (18mm) tack track is good enough, but Wray Schelin points out that a ½"(13mm) track gives better results. You can't argue when you see his panels in person.

How do you get good? Practice, practice, practice.

Books from Wolfgang Publications can be found at select book stores and numerous web sites.

Titles	ISBN	Price	# of pages
Advanced Airbrush Art	9781929133208	$27.95	144 pages
Advanced Custom Motorcycle Assembly & Fabrication	9781929133239	$27.95	144 pages
Advanced Custom Motorcycle Wiring - *Revised*	9781935828761	$27.95	144 pages
Advanced Pinstripe Art	9781929133321	$27.95	144 pages
Advanced Sheet Metal Fab	9781929133123	$27.95	144 pages
Advanced Tattoo Art - *Revised*	9781929133822	$27.95	144 pages
Airbrush How-To with Mickey Harris	9781929133505	$27.95	144 pages
Barris: Flames, Scallops and Striping	9781929133550	$24.95	144 pages
Bean're - Motorcycle Nomad	9781935828709	$18.95	256 pages
Body Painting	9781929133666	$27.95	144 pages
Building Hot Rods	9781929133437	$27.95	144 pages
Colorful World of Tattoo Models	9781935828716	$34.95	144 pages
Composite Materials 1	9781929133765	$27.95	144 pages
Composite Materials 2	9781929133932	$27.95	144 pages
Composite Materials 3	9781935828662	$27.95	144 pages
Composite Materials Step by Step Projects	9781929133369	$27.95	144 pages
Cultura Tattoo Sketchbook	9781935828839	$32.95	284 pages
Custom Bike Building Basics	9781935828624	$24.95	144 pages
Custom Motorcycle Fabrication	9781935828792	$27.95	144 pages
George the Painter	9781935828815	$18.95	256 pages
Harley-Davidson Sportster Hop-Up & Customizing Guide	9781935828952	$27.95	144 pages
Harley-Davidson Sportser Buell Engine Hop-Up Guide	9781929133093	$24.95	144 pages
How Airbrushes Work	9781929133710	$24.95	144 pages
Honda Enthusiast Guide Motorcycles 1959-1985	9781935828853	$27.95	144 pages
How-To Airbrush, Pinstripe & Goldleaf	9781935828693	$27.95	144 pages
How-To Airbrush Pin-ups	9781929133802	$27.95	144 pages
How-To Build Old Skool Bobber - 2nd Edition	9781935828785	$27.95	144 pages

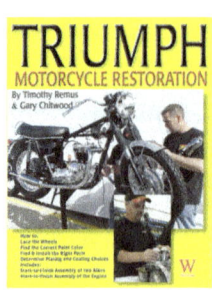
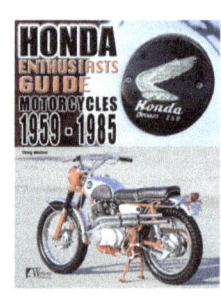

Books from Wolfgang Publications can be found at select book stores and numerous web sites.

Titles	ISBN	Price	# of pages
How-To Build a Cheap Chopper	9781929133178	$27.95	144 pages
How-To Build Cafe Racer	9781935828730	$27.95	144 pages
How-To Chop Tops	9781929133499	$24.95	144 pages
How-To Draw Monsters	9781935828914	$27.95	144 pages
How-To Fix American V-Twin	9781929133727	$27.95	144 pages
How-To Paint Tractors & Trucks	9781929133475	$27.95	144 pages
Hot Rod Wiring	9781929133987	$27.95	144 pages
Into the Skin	9781935828174	$34.95	144 pages
Kosmoski's *New* Kustom Paint Secrets	9781929133833	$27.95	144 pages
Learning the English Wheel	9781935828891	$27.95	144 pages
Mini Ebooks - Butterfly and Roses	9781935828167	Ebook Only	
Mini Ebooks - Skulls & Hearts	9781935828198	Ebook Only	
Mini Ebooks - Lettering & Banners	9781935828204	Ebook Only	
Mini Ebooks - Tribal Stars	9781935828211	Ebook Only	
Pin-Ups on Two Wheels	9781929133956	$29.95	144 pages
Pro Pinstripe	9781929133925	$27.95	144 pages
Sheet Metal Bible	9781929133901	$29.95	176 pages
Sheet Metal Fab Basics B&W	9781929133468	$24.95	144 pages
Sheet Metal Fab for Car Builders	9781929133383	$27.95	144 pages
SO-CAL Speed Shop, Hot Rod Chassis	9781935828860	$27.95	144 pages
Tattoo Bible #1	9781929133840	$27.95	144 pages
Tattoo Bible #2	9781929133857	$27.95	144 pages
Tattoo Bible #3	9781935828754	$27.95	144 pages
Tattoo Lettering Bible	9781935828921	$27.95	144 pages
Tattoo Sketchbook / Nate Power	9781935828884	$27.95	144 pages
Tattoo Sketchbook, Jim Watson	9781935828037	$32.95	112 pages
Triumph Restoration - Pre Unit	9781929133635	$29.95	144 pages
Triumph Restoration - Unit 650cc	9781929133420	$29.95	144 pages
Vintage Dirt Bikes - Enthusiast's Guide	9781929133314	$27.95	144 pages
Ult Sheet Metal Fab	9780964135895	$24.95	144 pages
Ultimate Triumph Collection	9781935828655	$49.95	144 pages

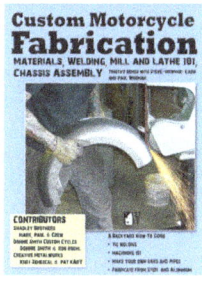  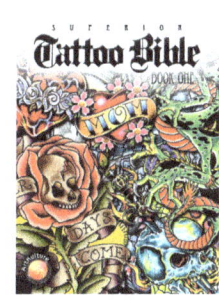  

Resources

Baileigh Industrial Tools
www.baileighindustrial.com

Dave Byron, *Spence Industries*
Spenceindustries98@gmail.com

Tommy Caruso, *Contour Metalshaping*
www.contourmetalshaping.com

Jack Charles, *Lakeside Technical College*
william.charles@gotoltc.edu

Jamie Downie, *Kustom Garage*
www.kustomgarage.com.au

Stan Fulton, *Fulton Metal Works*
sfulton@casscomm.com

David Gardiner
(Highly recommended shaping video.)
www.metalshapingzone.com

Jeb Greenstone, *Cutworm Customs*
www.cutwormspecialties.com

Kyle Yocum
Yocum's Signature Hot Rods
www.Yocumsrodshop.com

Mark Gerisch
Academy for the Art of Metal Shaping
(Highly recommended power hammer instruction.)
www.aametalshaping.com

Ron Covell
www.covell.biz

Ron Fournier
www.FournierEnterprises.com

Andrew Geelhoed, *Precision Guesswork*,
geelhoeds@hotmail.com

Craig Naff
Woodstock, Virginia

Mark Naglich, *Lakeside Rod and Custom*
360-871-1185

Austin Paruch, *Paruch Automotive Craftsmanship*
Austin-Lee@hotmail.com

Mike Phillips, *Phillips Hot Rod & Customs*
www.phillipsautomotiverepair.com

Chris Rusch RMD
www.rmdbenders.com

Wray Schelin
www.proshaper.com

Mike Wagner, *Cornfield Customs*
Cornfield_customs@hotmail.com

Kent White
www.tinmantech.com

Textbook Terms and Industry Language as it Pertains to Power Hammers

Stack Shrinking also known as tuck shrinking; is done with a specific die set that features a matching top to bottom die, one with a male wedge shape on the bottom, and a female shape on the top die. When a sheet of metal is run into the dies it creates a V shape in the top of the panel, when it is pulled back out by the operator the V is crushed down into the metal and at the same time it creates a shrink in the metal pulling it together and pushing it into the metal, making it thicker like cold forging

Lancaster die shrinking; this type of shrinking is usually used in a hand or kick shrinker that pushes the metal together. It is used more for flanges, edges, sweep creation or anywhere that is not likely to be welded

Annealing; is most commonly used on aluminum to soften it when it becomes work hardened.

Stretch; with a radiused die in the lower holder of the hammer, with a flat upper die, you can induce lift in the panel called shape. This can go from a very light crown to an extremely radical high crown like the ones found on a Cobra 427. The term can also refer to a linear die used in the lower holder of the hammer to create a reverse panel.

Shape; is something you get from shrinking or stretching a panel.

Form; happens when you already have the shape you wish in the panel but through hand manipulation the panel can be bent to fit your buck without any more shape going into the panel.

Flow; relates to the light lines reflected from the metal surface, useful in detecting and eliminating facets in the panel or between one panel to another.

Linear stretching; commonly means that the lower die used to make reverses in a panel is nearly flat with rounded edges and run off the edge of a panel to stretch the panel in the opposite direction to the rest of the panel.

Radial stretching; refers to the blow pattern created by a round die of varying radius that contacts the surface of the panel used in a power hammer. It sends out a ripple-like effect in the panel much like a pebble dropped in the water.

Power stroke; this term refers to the amount of force you can dial into the strike of the die against the panel to create shape.

Die height adjustment; differs from one hammer to the next depending on the manufacturer, but relates to the adjustment between the upper and lower dies for more or less wipe action when striking the panel.

Speed control; hammers like the MH-19 or MH-37HD, available through Baileigh Industrial, have a separate dial control that adjusts the speed of the motor driving the hammer.

Foot peddle; this is the main control that engages the hammer's action - works in tandem with the speed control dial.

Rubber top die; a very unique die tool that can be used in either the top or bottom tool holder of the power hammer, coupled with an opposing higher crown steal die. This can be used to put massive shape in a panel very quickly for raising a blister on the surface of the panel without affecting the sides of the panel which normally happens when you use a sand bag or stump for shrinking. In the same breath you can also shrink the panel just by moving to the edges of the panel to shrink around the edges.

No Fly Zones; areas of the panel being worked, where you want no shape at all.

Road Test a Power Hammer or English Wheel at Road America

If you want to learn how car bodies are made, now's your chance! AAMS, The Academy for the Art of Metal Shaping, is pleased to announce its new partnership with Road America. Starting in the 2015 season, The Academy for The Art Of Metal Shaping will maintain a pavilion on the RA infield fully stocked with the latest professional metal shaping tools available.

Next time you're at a race come on over and get some free hands-on instruction on the art of coachbuilding from one of our team members.

Whether you're a rookie, or pro, we'll introduce you to power hammers, English wheels, and many other tools used to turn aluminum and steel sheet into fast and fabulous car panels.

The AAMS/Road America Sheet Metal Pavilion is open during all Road America events. Don't miss it! Just show up with your enthusiasm and we'll do the rest. *Race cars don't just happen, they're built!*

www.aametalshaping.com
classes@aametalshaping.com

www.ingramcontent.com/pod-product-compliance
Lightning Source LLC
Chambersburg PA
CBHW081421230426
43668CB00016B/2304